Stories of the

Lewis R. Freeman

Alpha Editions

This edition published in 2024

ISBN : 9789362929037

Design and Setting By
Alpha Editions
www.alphaedis.com
Email - info@alphaedis.com

As per information held with us this book is in Public Domain.
This book is a reproduction of an important historical work. Alpha Editions uses the best technology to reproduce historical work in the same manner it was first published to preserve its original nature. Any marks or number seen are left intentionally to preserve its true form.

Contents

I. STORIES OF THE SHIPS THE
STORY OF THE *CORNWALL* .... - 1 -

THE STORY OF THE *SYDNEY* .... - 27 -

II. LIFE IN THE FLEET A
BATTLESHIP AT SEA .... - 54 -

A NORTH SEA SWEEP .... - 66 -

A VISIT TO THE BRITISH FLEET .... - 81 -

THE HEALTH OF THE FLEET .... - 88 -

ECONOMY IN THE GRAND FLEET .... - 93 -

CHRISTMAS IN A "HAPPY" SHIP .... - 102 -

IN A BALLOON SHIP .... - 107 -

COALING THE GRAND FLEET .... - 114 -

THE STOKERS .... - 123 -

"GETTING TOGETHER" .... - 136 -

I. STORIES OF THE SHIPS

THE STORY OF THE *CORNWALL*

I. PLYMOUTH TO THE FALKLANDS

Of the countless stories of naval action which I have listened to in the course of the months I have spent with the Grand Fleet, I cannot recall a single one which was told as the consequence of being asked for with malice aforethought. I have never yet found a man of action who was enamoured of the sound of his own voice raised in the recital of his own exploits, and if there is one thing more than another calculated to throw an otherwise not untalkative British Naval Officer into a state of uncommunicativeness, in comparison with which the traditional silence of the sphinx or the proverbial close-mouthedness of the clam are alike sheer garrulity, it is to ask him, point blank, to tell you (for instance) how he took his submarine into the Baltic, or what his destroyer did at Jutland, or how he fought his cruiser at Dogger Bank, or something similar.

The quiet-voiced but always interesting and often dramatic recitals of such things as these which I have heard have invariably been led up to quite incidentally—at dinner, on the bridge or quarter-deck, around the wardroom fire, or through something else that has just been told. Several times I have found in officers' diaries—little records never meant for other eyes than those of the writers' own friends or families—which have been turned over to me to verify some point regarding which I had inquired, laconic references to incidents and events of great human and even historic interest, and one of the most amusing and dramatic yarns I have ever listened to was told me in a "kite" balloon—plunging in the forty-mile wind against which it was being towed like a hooked salmon—by a man who had assured me before we went up that nothing really exciting had ever fallen to his experience.

It was in this way—an anecdote now and then as this or that incident of the day recalled it to his mind—that Captain —— came to tell me the story of the *Cornwall* during those eventful early months of the war when he commanded that now famous cruiser. He mentioned her first, I believe, one night in his cabin when, referring to a stormy midwinter month, most of which had been spent by his Division of the Grand Fleet on some sort of work at sea, I spoke of the "rather strenuous interval" we had experienced.

"If you think life in a battleship of the Grand Fleet strenuous," laughed the Captain, extending himself comfortably in his armchair before the glowing grate, "I wonder what you would have thought of the life we led in the old *Cornwall*. Not very far from a hundred and twenty thousand miles of steaming was her record for the first two years of the war, and in that time she ploughed most of the Seven Seas and coasted in the waters of all but one of the Six Continents. Always on the lookout for something or other, coaling as we could, provisioning as we might—let me tell you that coming to the Grand Fleet after that (at least until a few months had elapsed and the contrast wore off) was like retiring on a pension in comparison."

He settled himself deeper into the soft upholstery, extended his feet nearer the fire, lighted a fresh cigar, and, in the hour which elapsed before the evening mail came aboard, told me of the work of the *Cornwall* in those first chaotic weeks of the war which preceded the battle of the Falklands.

"We were at Plymouth when the war began," said he, "and our first work was in connexion with protecting and 'shepherding' safely to port several British ships carrying bullion which were still on the high seas. It was a baffling sort of a job, especially as there were two or three German raiders loose in the North Atlantic, the favourite ruse of each of which was to represent itself as a British cruiser engaged in the same benevolent work the *Cornwall* was on. Warned of these 'wolves-in-shepherds'-clothing,' the merchantmen we sought to protect were afraid to reveal their whereabouts by wireless, the consequence being that our first forerunning efforts to safeguard the seas resolved themselves into a sort of marine combination of 'Blind-Man's Buff' and 'Hide-and-Seek,' played pretty well all over the Atlantic. All the ships with especially valuable cargoes got safely to port ultimately, though none of them, that I recall, directly under the wing of the *Cornwall*. It was our first taste of the 'So-near-and-yet-so-far' kind of life that is the inevitable lot of the cruiser which essays the dual rôle of 'Commerce Protector' and 'Raider Chaser.'

"After a few hours at 'Gib,' we were next sent across to Casa Blanca, where the appearance of the *Cornwall* was about the first tangible evidence that French Africa had of the fact that England was really coming into the war in earnest. There was a good deal of unrest in Morocco at the time, for the Germans were even then at work upon their insidious propaganda among the Moslems of all the colonies of the Allies. The 'buzz' in the bazaars that the appearance of a British warship started must have served a very useful purpose at this critical juncture in carrying to the Arabs of the interior word that France was not going to have to stand alone against Germany. Our reception by both the French and native population of Casa Blanca was most enthusiastic, and during all of our stay a cheering procession followed in the wake of every party of officers or men who went ashore.

"Leaving Casa Blanca, we were sent back to the Atlantic to search for commerce destroyers, ultimately working south by the Canaries and Cape Verde Islands to South American waters, where the *Karlsruhe* was then at the zenith of her activities. The chase of this enterprising and elusive raider, whose career was finally brought to an inglorious end by her going aground on a West Indian Island, kept the *Cornwall*—along with a number of other British cruisers—steadily on the move, until the ominous and painful news of the destruction of Craddock's fleet off Coronel suddenly brought us face to face with the fact that there was soon going to be bigger game than a lone pirate to be stalked.

"We never had the luck to sight even so much as the smoke of the *Karlsruhe*, although—as I only learned too late to take advantage of the information—the *Cornwall* was within an hour or two's steaming of her on one occasion. I *did* think we had her once, though—a jolly amusing incident it was, too. I was getting uncomfortably short of food at the time—a very common experience in the 'here-to-day-and-gone-to-morrow' sort of life we were leading;—so that when the welcome news reached me by wireless one morning that a British ship—Buenos Aires to New York with frozen beef—was due to pass through the waters we were then patrolling, I lost no time in heading over to intercept her on the chance of doing a bit of marketing.

"We picked her up promptly as reckoned, but, while she was still hull down on the horizon, her skipper began to signal frantically, '*I am being chased by the "Karlsruhe"!*' Here was luck indeed. I ordered 'Action Stations' to be sounded, and the course of the ship to be altered toward the point where I figured the smoke of the pursuing pirate would begin to smudge the sky-line as she came swooping down upon her prey. Sighting nothing after holding on this course for a while, I came to the conclusion that the raider must be hidden by the impenetrable smoke-pall with which the flying beef-ship had masked a wide arc of the western horizon, and headed up in that direction, begging the fugitive in the meantime to give me the bearing of her pursuer as accurately as possible.

"Her only reply to this, however, was to belch out 'smoke-screen' faster than ever and continue rending the empyrean ether with renewed '*I am being chased by the "Karlsruhe"!*' In vain I assured her that we were the H.M.S. *Cornwall*, and would take the greatest delight in seeing that the chase was put an end to, if she would only tell us from which direction the *Karlsruhe* was coming, and cease to throw out a bituminous blanket for the enemy to hide behind. Blacker and blacker rolled the smoke, heavier and heavier piled the screen to leeward, and still more frantically shrilled the appeals for help. At the end of my patience at actions which it now began to dawn upon me looked more than a little suspicious, I headed the *Cornwall* straight after the runaway and soon reduced the interval separating us sufficiently to reach her with 'Visual.' She brought up sharp at my 'Stop instantly!' and a quarter of an hour later my boarding party was clambering over her side.

"'Where's the *Karlsruhe*?' I shouted impatiently to the Boarding Officer as his boat came back alongside again. I knew something of the accuracy of German long range naval gunnery, and was far from being easy in mind regarding the kind of surprise packet that might at any moment be wafted out of that slowly thinning smoke-blur to leeward.

"'There,' he replied with a comprehensive sweep of the arm in quite the opposite direction from the one I had been expecting the enemy. 'Right there, Sir.' That old lunatic of a skipper thought the *Cornwall* was the *Karlsruhe*!"

"Did you get your frozen beef?" I asked.

The Captain smiled the pleased smile of one who recalls something that has given him great satisfaction.

"I think that afternoon marked the beginning of the 'Food Economy' campaign in the Navy," he replied. "If the Admiralty had been able to continue buying frozen beef at the rate that crestfallen but highly relieved skipper—quite of his own free will—charged for the lot we loaded up after he had found it was not to be his fate to be sunk by the *Karlsruhe*,—well, the Government could have probably built a new battleship or two and never missed the money out of the saving."

The recollection of the treat that fresh meat was after a long period on "bully beef" ration turned the Captain's thoughts to another time of plenty he had experienced after the *Cornwall* had helped the wounded *Carmania* limp back to Base following her successful engagement with the *Cap Trafalgar*.

"In these times of food economy and restricted rations," he said, "it fairly makes my mouth water to think of the feasts Captain G—— spread for us during the days we were devising a way to get the battered *Carmania* back to England. You see, when the war started she was just about to sail on one of her transatlantic voyages with the usual midsummer cargo of American millionaires, and her cuisine was of a character calculated to satisfy their Epicurean tastes. When they converted her to an auxiliary cruiser, it was the usual sledge-hammer, crow-bar, and over-the-side procedure with the mirrors, the upholsteries, and the mahoganies, but they left the stores, God bless them, they left the stores. Can you fancy how things such as truffled quail, and asparagus tips with mayonnaise—*iced*—and *café parfait*, and Muscat dates, and California oranges—with the big gold labels on—tasted to men who had been for weeks pretty nearly down to the classic old windjammer ration of 'lobscouse' and 'dog's-body'? And those plump, black, five-inch-long Havanas in the silver foil (I can smell the soothing fumes of them yet), and that rarely blended Mocha, and those bottles of 1835 Cognac—the pungent bouquet of them scents the memories of the long evenings I sat with G—— in the wreck of his fire-swept cabin while he yarned to me of the ripping fight he had just come out of. And how we all envied G—— his luck—getting as sporting a show as a man could ask for in that half-converted liner while we cruisers were vainly chasing smoke and rumours over most of the South Atlantic. Nothing less than the banquets he gave us would have salved our heart-burnings."

And so it was that the Captain was led on to speak of what he had heard—from those who took part in it, and only a few hours from the time it happened—of the first great duel ever fought between modern armed merchantmen, a conflict, indeed, which is still practically unique in naval history.

"There was not much to choose between the ships," he said. "The *Cap Trafalgar*—one of the latest of the Hamburg Sud Amerika liners—had a good deal the best of it on the score of age, and the *Carmania* probably something on the score of size. The latter had been hastily converted at Liverpool immediately after the outbreak of the war, while the former turned herself from sheep into wolf about the same time by arming herself with the guns of a small German gun-boat. This craft, by the way, steamed to the nearest Brazilian port and, with true Hunnish logic, claimed the right to intern as a peaceful German Merchantman on the strength of the fact that it was no longer armed! The largest guns that either ship had were four-inch, the *Carmania* having slight advantage on the score of number. The *Carmania* would have been no match for the *Karlsruhe*, just as the *Cap Trafalgar* would have fallen easy prey to the *Cornwall* or another of the British cruisers in those waters. Under the circumstances, it was a happy fatality that let these two ex-floating palaces fight with each other and in their own class.

"The first word we had of the engagement was a wireless Captain G—— sent out saying, in effect, that he had sunk the *Trafalgar*, but, as his bridge was burned up, his steering gear shot away, and all his navigating instruments destroyed, that he would be glad to have some one come and tell him where he was and lead him to a place where he could, so to speak, lie down and lick his wounds for a while. It took a jolly good bit of searching to find a ship that couldn't tell any more about itself than that, but we finally sighted her ragged silhouette and gave her a lead to such a haven as the practically open seas of our rendezvous afforded.

"Poor G—— had lost a good deal more than his steering gear it soon transpired, for the fire which had consumed his bridge had also gutted his cabin, and reduced everything in it to cinders except an old Norfolk jacket. How *that* escaped we never could figure out, for of garments hanging on pegs to the left and right of it no trace was left. As G—— was of about three times the girth of any other British officer in those waters at the time, the wardrobe we tried to get together for him was a grotesque combination; indeed, so far as I recall now, the old Norfolk had to serve him as everything from pyjamas and bath-robe to dinner-jacket and great-coat during that trying period. It was a weird figure he cut presiding at those Gargantuan feasts he spread for us on the bruised and battered old *Carmania*, but there wasn't a one of us who wouldn't have changed places with him—Norfolk and all—for the assurance of half his luck. Such is the monotony of this patrol work in the outer seas, that, after your first enthusiasm wears off, you get into a state of mind in which you can never conceive that anything is ever going to happen. That we had the one most decisive naval battle of the war just ahead of us, no one dreamed at this time.

"The fight between the *Carmania* and *Cap Trafalgar*," he continued, "has well been called 'The Battle of the Haystacks,' for never before (or since, for that matter) have two ships with such towering upper works stood off and tried to batter each other to pieces with gunfire. Indeed, I well recall G——'s saying that, up to the very end, he could not conceive that either ship could sink the other, and of how—even after the *Carmania* had been struck three or four-score times and a raging fire forward had driven him from the bridge—he kept wondering in the back of his brain what sort of a fight the duel would resolve itself into when both had exhausted their shells. Luckily, he did not have to face that problem.

"Both ships, according to G——'s account, began blazing at each other as soon as they came in range, and, as each was eager to fight it out to a finish, the distance separating them was, for a while, reduced as rapidly as possible. At something like three thousand yards, however, some sort of a rapid-fire gun burst into action on the *Trafalgar*. 'It didn't appear to be doing me much harm,' said G—— in telling of it, 'but the incessant "pom-pom" of the accursed thing got so much on my nerves that I drew off far enough to dull the edge of its infernal yapping.'

"A thing which came near to putting the *Carmania* out of the running before she had completed the polishing off of her opponent was the shell which I have spoken of as violating the sanctity of the Captain's cabin—the one that burned everything but the Norfolk jacket. This projectile—a four-inch—though (probably owing to the small resistance offered by the light upper works) it did not explode, generated enough heat in its passage to start a fire. Beginning on G——'s personal effects, this conflagration spread to the bridge, destroying the navigating instruments and ultimately making it impossible to remain there—the latter a serious blow in itself. What made this fire especially troublesome was the difficulty, because of the cutting of the main, of bringing water to bear upon it. As it was, it was necessary to head the *Carmania* 'down the wind' to reduce the draught fanning the flames. Nothing else would have saved her. Except for one thing, this expedient would have enabled the now thoroughly worsted (though G—— didn't know it) *Trafalgar* to withdraw from the action, and this was that the latter was herself on fire and had to take the same course willy-nilly. From that moment on the battle was as irretrievably joined as one of those old Spanish knife-duels in which the opponents were locked together in a room to fight to a finish. Often as not, so they say, the victor in one of these fights only survived the loser by minutes or hours, and so would it have been in this instance had they not finally been able to extinguish the fire on the *Carmania*.

"G——'s account of the way he had to carry on after being driven from the bridge—it was really a splendid bit of seamanship—was funny in the extreme, but the reality must have been funnier still, that is, if that term can be applied to anything happening while shells are bursting and blowing men to bits every few seconds. G—— is one of the biggest men in the Navy—around the waist, I mean—so it wasn't to be expected of him to be very shifty on his feet. And yet, by the irony of Fate, it was he of all men who was suddenly confronted with a task that required only less 'foot-work' than it did 'head-work.' With the battle going on all the time, they rigged up some sort of a 'jury' steering gear, or it may be that they steered her by her screws. At any rate, G—— had to con her from the most commanding position he could find on one of the after decks, or rather, as he had no longer voice-pipe communication with the engine-room, he had to keep dashing back and forth (it must have been for all the world like a batsman running in cricket) between two or three commanding positions. 'If I wanted to open the range a bit,' he said, 'I had to nip for'ard, wait till there was an interval in both gun-fire and shell-burst, and yell down a hatchway' (or was it a ventilator?) 'to the engine-room to "Slow port!" or if I suddenly found it imperative to open the distance, I had to make the same journey and pass the word down to "Stop starboard!" The very thought of that mad shuttling back and forth under the equatorial sun used to make poor G—— mop his forehead and pour himself a fresh drink every time he told the story.

"Battered and burning fiercely as both ships were, G—— confessed that even at this juncture he could not rid himself of the feeling that neither of them had enough shells to sink the other. 'I was racking my brain for some plan of action to follow when that moment arrived,' he said, 'when suddenly the *Trafalgar* began to heel sharply and started to sink. It was our second or third salvo, which had holed her badly at the water-line, that did the business. She had kept steaming and fighting for close to an hour and a quarter afterwards, though.'

"G—— told us one very good story about his Gunnery officer. 'It was just before the shell which started the fire struck us,' he said, 'that Y——'s sun helmet was knocked off—I don't remember whether it was by the wind or the concussion of the firing. Seeing it fall to the deck below, he ran to the rail of the bridge and began shouting for some one to bring it back to him. Before long, luckily, a seaman who had heard the shouting in a lull of the firing, poked his head out to see what it was about, and presently came puffing up the ladder with the fugitive head-piece. I say *luckily*, because the gun-control for the whole ship was suspended while Y—— waited for that infernal helmet. And the funniest thing about it all was that, when I ventured to suggest a few days later that it might be well if he made use of the chin-strap of his helmet the next time he was in action, he claimed to have no recollection whatever of the incident—thought he had been "sticking to his guns" all the time. Just shows how a man's brain works in air-tight compartments when he is really busy.'

"The Surgeon of the *Carmania* (continued the Captain)—a splendid chap who had given up a lucrative West-end practice and sworn he was under forty (although he was really fifty-two) in order to get a chance to do something for his country—told me many stories to prove the splendid spirit of the men that passed under his hands during and after the fight. Though most of the crew were only Royal Naval Reservists, with no experience of and but little training for fighting, it appears that they stood what is perhaps the hardest of all trials—that of seeing their mates wounded and killed beside them—like seasoned veterans.

"'There was one stout-hearted young Cockney,' said the Surgeon, 'whom, after I had finished removing a number of shell fragments from various parts of his anatomy, I asked what he thought of the fight. "Rippin', Sir," he replied, grinning ecstatically through the bandage that held up the flap of a torn cheek; "rippin', never been in one like it before." Then, as his eye caught the smile which I could not quite repress at the lifetime of naval battling suggested by that "nev'r afore," he concluded with "Not ev'n in Whitechapel."'

"The Surgeon came across one man who insisted that the blood flowing from a ragged tear in his arm was really spattered there when one of his mates—whose mangled body he bestrode—had been decapitated by a shell a few minutes before; and there was one lot of youngsters who went on cheerily 'Yo-heave-ho-ing' in hoisting some badly needed shells which were so slippery with blood that they had to be sanded before they could be handled. Grimly pathetic was the story he told me of a gunner whose torn hand he had just finished amputating and bandaging when some one shouted into the door of the dressing station that the *Trafalgar* was going down.

"'He crowded to a port I had had opened,' said the Surgeon, 'just in time to see one of the last salvoes from the *Carmania* go crashing into the side of the heeling enemy. "Huroor, boys," he shouted; "give 'em beans," and as he cheered he started (what had evidently been a favourite gesture of approval and excitement with him) to smite mightily with his right fist into the palm of his left hand. But the blow fell upon air; there was no answering thwack. The gnarled, weather-beaten fist shot past a bandaged stump. He drew back with surprise for a moment, and then, grinning a bit sheepishly, like a boy surprised in some foolish action, edged back beside me at the port. "Quite forgot there was su'thin' missin'," he said half apologetically, trying to wriggle the elbow of the maimed arm back into the sling from which it had slipped. "S'pose I'll be havin' to get used to it, won't I?" As the *Trafalgar* took a new list and began rapidly to settle he burst into renewed "Huroors." "By Gawd, Sir," he cried, when she had finally gone, "if I 'ad as many 'ands as an oktypuss, I'd 'a giv'n 'em all fer the joy o' puttin' that blinkin' pyrit down to Davy Jones."'"

The Captain gazed long at the coals of the grate, on his face the pleased smile of one who recalls treasured memories. "I can't tell you how sorry we were to see the *Carmania* go," he said finally. "My word, how we *did* enjoy those feasts good old G—— spread for us!" With a laugh he roused himself from the pleasant reverie and took up again the narrative of the *Cornwall*.

"The first intimation we had" (he resumed) "of the sinking of Admiral Craddock's fleet came in the form of a wireless from the *Defence* asking if I had heard of the disaster at Coronel. Details which came in the course of the next day or two brought home to us the astonishing change in the whole situation which the appearance of Von Spee in South American waters had wrought. The blow fell like a bolt from the blue.

"As rapidly as possible the various British warships in the South Atlantic rendezvoused off Montevideo to discuss a plan of action. What the next move of the victorious Von Spee would be we could only surmise. German prisoners picked up after the Falklands battle said his ultimate plan—after seizing Port Stanley for a base, and undergoing such a refit there as was practicable with the means at his disposal—was to scatter his ships as commerce raiders all over the Atlantic, cutting, if possible, the main sea arteries of England to North America. The Germans figured, according to these prisoners, that the suspension of the North Atlantic traffic for even a month (no impossible thing for five speedy cruisers in the light of the delays to sailings caused by the *Emden* and *Karlsruhe* working alone) would practically paralyse England's war efforts and reduce her military effort in France to almost negligible proportions. I am much more inclined to believe that this—rather than escorting a fleet of German merchantmen, bearing German reservists from Argentina, Uruguay, and Southern Brazil, to South-West Africa from Buenos Aires and Montevideo—was the real plan of Von Spee.

However, it was the immediate rather than the ultimate plans of the Germans that was our chief—in fact, our only—concern. Whether Von Spee intended heading for the North Atlantic later or South Africa, or up the Thames—the only way he could clear the road to any of these objectives was by first destroying such British warships as still remained in South American waters. It was these ships which had hurried to get together off Montevideo, in order to make the path of the enemy as thorny and full of pitfalls as possible.

"They had no illusions respecting what the immediate future held for them, that little group of cruiser captains that gathered in the Admiral's cabin of the *Defence* to formulate a plan of action. We knew nothing at that time of what had been decided upon at the Admiralty; indeed, we were quite in agreement that it would be deemed inexpedient to send any battle cruisers away from the North Sea, where they might be imperatively needed any day, on a voyage to the South Atlantic that might easily resolve itself into a months'-long wild-goose chase. Our plans, therefore, were laid entirely on the assumption that we should have to do the best we could with the ships already available.

"There was not a man of us who was not keen on the chance of a fight at even the prohibitive odds under which it appeared inevitable that the one ahead of us must be fought, but the prospects of success were anything but alluring. Every day that passed had brought reports revealing the completeness of the enemy's victory at Coronel, and all of these were more than confirmed when the *Glasgow*—whose captain had had the good sense to retire from a battle in which there was no longer a chance for him to be of any use—came in and joined us.

"It would be easy to suggest conditions under which one naval force, faced by another as much stronger than itself as the Germans were than the British at this time, would be justified in avoiding an action. The present was not such an occasion, however; in fact, I don't think it ever occurred to any of us to bring up a discussion of that phase of the question at all. This, briefly, was the way the matter presented itself to us: The measure of the power of the Germans to inflict harm to the Allies was their supply of shells. These gone—always provided no new supply reached them—the menace, even though the ships were yet unsunk, was practically at an end. We knew that they had already used up a considerable quantity of their munition in a foolish bombardment of the little tropical port of Papeete, in the French Societies, and we knew that a very large amount had been expended at Coronel. They still probably had enough, we figured, to see them through many months of commerce raiding if only they could avoid another general action against warships, and such an action, even if it was a losing one from our standpoint, it was our manifest rôle to provoke, and at the earliest possible moment.

"This point decided, about all that remained to be considered was how to make the most effective disposition of such ships as we had at our disposal when once the enemy was in sight. We knew just what ships we would have to meet. We also knew, practically to a gun, how they were armed. Moreover, with Coronel as an object lesson, we knew how well those ships were handled, and with what deadly effectiveness those guns were served. Now that it is all ancient history, I think there is no reason why I should not tell you how we arranged that our ships should 'take partners' for the little 'sea-dance' they were expecting to shake their heels at.

"The *Defence*—an armoured cruiser of the *Minotaur* type, subsequently sunk at Jutland—was to tackle the *Scharnhorst*, Von Spee's flagship. The former was the only ship we had that was anywhere nearly a match for either of the larger German cruisers. She exceeded them in displacement by several thousand tons, and her four nine-point-twos and ten seven-point-fives had a comfortable margin of metal over that fired from the *Scharnhorst's* eight eight-point-twos and six five-point-nines. In a fair duel with either of the larger Germans, I think there is little doubt she would have had the best of it. In the battle we expected to go into, however, there could be no certainty that she was going to be able to give her undivided attention to the *vis-à-vis* we had picked for her during a sufficient interval to finish up the job.

"The *Carnarvon* and the *Cornwall* were to be given the formidable task of keeping the *Gneisenau* so busy that she could not help her sister fight the *Defence*. Our combined displacement was about equal to that of our prospective opponent, but the four seven-point-fives and twenty six-inch (all we had between us) could hardly have prevented her pounding us to pieces with her eight-point-twos, in the event that she elected to use her speed to keep beyond the effective range of our lighter guns. By dashing into close range we might have had a chance with her, or, again there was the possibility we might lead her a dance that would take her out of the way long enough to give the *Defence* time to finish polishing off the *Scharnhorst*, in which event the former might have been able to intervene in our favour.

"Small as would have been our chance of carrying through our part of the programme successfully, the *Gneisenau* was the one opponent I desired above all the others, on account of the way I knew it would buck up the ship's company to feel that they were having a whack at the ship that sunk the *Monmouth*. There were a good many men in the *Monmouth* who had gone to her from the *Cornwall*, and our men never tired cursing the Hun for letting their mates drown at Coronel without making any effort to save them. They had something to say on that score when their turn came at the Falklands.

"The *Glasgow* we were going to give a chance to wipe out her Coronel score by sending her in against the *Nürnberg*. With her superior speed, and her two six-inch and ten four-inch guns against the latter's ten four-point ones, she would probably have had the best of what could not but have been a very pretty fight if no one had interfered with it. Here again, unluckily, the chances were against a duel to the finish. Against the *Dresden*—a very worthy sister of the *Emden*—the very best we could muster was the armed merchantman, *Orama*. This (unless another armed merchantman—the *Otranto*, which had escaped with the *Glasgow* from Coronel—became available) left us nothing to oppose to the *Leipzig*, which, in that event, would have been a sort of a 'rover,' free to bestow her attention and shells wherever they appeared likely to do the most harm. And (from the way she was fought at the Falklands, where she was my 'opposite number') let me tell you that a jolly troublesome 'rover' she would have been.

"That, in a few words, was our little plan for making Von Spee use up the remainder of his ammunition. That was our principal object, and there can be no doubt that we would have come pretty near complete success in attaining it. For the rest, you can judge for yourself what our chances would have been. As the Fates would have it, however, that battle was never to be fought, save on paper in the Admiral's cabin of the old *Defence*. Before ever we had completed preparations for our 'magazine-emptying' sally against Von Spee, word was winged to us that the Admiralty had a plan of its own in process of incubation, and that we were to standby to co-operate.

"Sturdee and his battle cruisers were well on their way to the South Atlantic, however, before even an inkling of what was afoot was vouchsafed us, and even then my orders were simply to rendezvous with him at the 'Base' I have spoken of before—the one where we foregathered and feasted with the *Carmania*. I breathed no word of where and why we were going until the muddy waters of the Plate estuary were left behind and the last least possibility of a 'leak' to the shore was out of the question.

Then I simply passed it on to the men by posting some word of it on the notice-board. There was no cheering, either then or even a few days later, when the *Inflexible* and the *Invincible*, the latter flying Admiral Sturdee's flag, came nosing in from the Atlantic and dropped anchor at the 'Base'; but the promise of action in the immediate future was like wine to the men. They were simply tumbling over themselves to carry out the most ordinary routine duties, and so it continued right up to the moment that Von Spee's foretops, gliding along above the low promontory of Port William, brought them to 'Action Stations' with real work to do at last.

"Sturdee had his plans all laid, and we repaired to the *Invincible* shortly after her arrival to familiarise ourselves with them. All in all, it wasn't so very different a gathering as that one which took place on the *Defence*, off Montevideo, to plan another battle—the one which was never to take place. I don't mind admitting though, that there was a bit more 'buoyancy' to the atmosphere of this second conference, the natural consequence of our 'improved prospects.' There is no use denying that it gives a man a more comfortable feeling to know that he is in a ship that has reasonable expectation of sending its 'opposite' to the bottom of the sea, than to be faced with the prospect of going out as a sort of animated lure to wheedle the enemy out of his shells.

"With the *Invincible* and *Inflexible* Sturdee had sufficient force to be able to dispense with the *Defence*, which was, I believe, sent to African water to join a force that was gathering there on the off-chance that the Germans slipped through the net that was being flung off South America. For scouting purposes, the *Bristol* and the *Kent*—both of which had foregathered with us at the 'Base'—were added to our 'punitive expedition,' which finally got under weigh for the Falklands on November 28. Steaming in a formation best calculated to sweep a wide range of seas, we held our southerly course for nine days, sighting, so far as I recall, no ship of any description except those of our own force. On the eighth day we weathered a heavy blizzard, but it was out of a clear dawn that the low, rounded hills of the Falklands—so suggestive in many respects of the Orkneys and the north of Scotland—took shape the following morning. We dropped anchor in the double harbour of Port William and Port Stanley at nine o'clock of the forenoon of December 7. Before another twenty-four hours had passed Von Spee—hurrying as though to a rendezvous—had made his appearance, and we were raising steam to go out and even up Craddock's account with him."

II. THE BATTLE OF THE FALKLANDS

The Captain had come for a breath of fresh air on the quarter-deck at the end of a grey winter's day, and it was the memories called up by the resemblance of the low, rounded, treeless hills which ringed the Northern Base to some other hills which he had good reason to carry a vivid mental picture of that set him talking of the Falklands.

"They're very much like these," he said, "those wind-swept hills around Port Stanley; indeed, I know of few other parts of the world so far apart geographically that have so much in common topographically and climatically. Their people, too, are a good deal like the northern Scots and Orcadians, with a dry sense of humour that usually manifests itself at your first meeting with them, when they tell you that the Falklands have two seasons, the cold and the snowy. The latter, they tell you,—because the snow stops up the chinks and keeps out the wind—is rather the warmer of the two. They are a sturdy, resolute lot, too, and we found that, quite expecting the coming of the German fleet and with no sure knowledge that British naval help would arrive in time, they had made all preparations to fight the enemy to the limit of their very primitive resources.

"And a jolly good fight they would have put up, too. The old *Canopus* (the battleship which did not come up in time to help Craddock at Coronel) had been grounded in the inner harbour and turned into a 'land fort.' Her heavy turret guns had been left aboard her, while those of her secondary batteries had been mounted at the most favourable positions on the hills. The 'standing army'—of something like thirty-five, I believe—had been recruited up to several times that figure, and all over the island firearms, ancient and modern, had been taken down and made ready for use. Von Spee's sailors and marines would have had many a ridge-to-ridge skirmish on their hands before they completed the conquest of the Falklands.

"The coming of Sturdee put an entirely different face on things," continued the Captain, smartly side-stepping the flying "grummet" which had been flicked across his path from out of a howling pack of flannelled "snotties" deep in the throes of hockey on the opposite side of the quarter-deck. "'When are the Huns coming?' was still the question on every tongue; but it was now put anticipatively rather than apprehensively. They had not long to wait.

"I shall never forget that morning they appeared. It was scarcely twenty hours from the time we had dropped anchor, and most of the ships of the squadron were rushing those odd and ends of cleaning up, overhauling, revictualling, and the like that always follow arrival in port. The *Cornwall*, with some repairs on one of her engines to be effected, was at six hours' notice, and the *Bristol*, for similar reasons, at somewhat longer. Only the *Kent* was ready to put to sea at once.

"I was in my bath when a signal reading 'Raise steam for full speed with all despatch' was handed me, and it did not need another signal, which arrived a few minutes later, to tell me that, by some amazing stroke of 'joss,' the enemy was near at hand. How near I did not dream until the guns of the old *Canopus* began to boom. Luckily, I was already shaved" (I liked that little touch), "but, even so, my finishing dressing and breakfasting within twelve minutes was a very creditable performance of its kind. I can't say much for the toilet I made, but the breakfast was a good hearty one, with porridge, eggs, and marmalade. With an action in the offing, and no knowing when you are going to have time to eat again, it is only common sense to fortify against an indefinite fast.

"By the time I reached the bridge the topmasts of an armoured and a light cruiser were visible, slipping along above the headland which cut off the harbour from the open sea. The events of the next few hours were to etch the profile of the latter ship indelibly upon my memory, for it was the *Leipzig*, coming up with the *Gneisenau* to destroy the Port Stanley Wireless Station. From the foretop of the *Canopus* they were able to see the Huns clearing for action; and the *Glasgow* and the *Bristol*, both of which were in the inner harbour, also had a clear view across the depressed neck of the peninsula. The other ships of the squadron saw no more than topmasts until they had raised steam and reached the open sea.

"Just how the Huns came to make the disconcerting discovery that there were modern battle cruisers concealed by the higher seaward end of the peninsula I learned from an officer who had been saved from the sinking *Gneisenau*, who told me the story in his guttural broken English. They had expected to find the *Canopus* at Port Stanley, he said, and perhaps the *Cornwall* and *Carnarvon* and other light cruisers; but anything of the class of the *Invincible* and *Inflexible*—'Mein Gott, Nein! Wen der Gunnery Ludenant sent word from der foredop down' (he sputtered) 'dot he zwei ships mit dreipodt madsts gesehen had, mein Kapdtin he say, "Nein, nein, es ist eempossibl. Ich will ein man mit der gut eyes up senden." Wen this man say, ya, he see zwei dreipodt madsts, mein Kapdtin, he say, "Der Teufel, now Ich must go quickt. Ein hour, zwei hour, we run, sehr schnell. Den komen aus der Inglish ships, und preddy soon Ich see dem komen mehr schell von uns." Den Ich say: "Mein Kapdtin, you must der mehr schnell gehen, or you must der fight machen." He say, "Ya, ya," und he mehr schnell try zu gehen. Nicht gut. No good. Den we up mit der *Scharnhorst* gekommen, und der Admiral, he say, "Nun will we der fight gemachen. Den we machen der fight. Nichts, no good. Kaput! Feenish!"'"

The Captain stopped at the windward end of the deck and let the breeze fan a brow that had grown red during his effort at literal rendition. A grin of pleased reminiscence sat on his face. "My word, but it must have given the Hun a jolly good jolt, that first sight of those 'dreipodt madsts!'" he explained finally, as he put on his cap and fell into step beside me again.

"If Von Spee ever had any time for *arrière pensée* before the sea closed over him," he resumed, "he must have reproached himself bitterly for not pushing on in force and attacking us in the harbour before we had steam up. If his whole squadron had come up as the *Gneisenau* and *Leipzig* did, they could undoubtedly have given us a very unpleasant hour or two while we were raising steam. We would have polished them off in the end, of course, but they would have done us a deal more harm than by the tactics they did follow. Again, there is a chance that, if the two armoured cruisers had pressed the attack alone—as they eventually were forced to do—they might have inflicted enough damage to our light cruisers to have made the escape of all three (instead of only one) of theirs a possibility. However, Von Spee's star of good fortune, which had been at its zenith at Coronel, was now sinking to near the horizon, and it was ordained that at the Falklands he should meet an enemy who was both faster and heavier armed than he, under conditions of sea and light which favoured him no whit.

"The battle of the Falklands was really won in the harbour of Port Stanley. It was all a question of how soon we could get out. If we could reach the enemy in anything like full force there was little doubt of the result. A delay of an hour or two, however, might have easily resulted in their scattering so effectually that the running down of the last of them would have been a matter of months, and months, too, marked with great losses of, and greater delays to, the merchant shipping of two hemispheres. Nothing short of the truly splendid efforts of the engine-room and stokehold personnel of Sturdee's ships would have given their gunners their chance to win the battle of the Falklands.

"Of the *Cornwall's* achievement in this respect I am especially proud. With one of the engines partially dismantled, we would have been doing all that was expected of us if we had been under full steam in six hours. Indeed, that was the very notice we had gone under, in order to do the overhauling desired. And now let me tell you what happened. It was ten minutes after eight when the signal to raise steam for full speed was received, and before half-past ten she was steaming out of the harbour. We could have got under weigh some minutes earlier than we did but for having to let the *Invincible* and the *Inflexible*, which had been lying inshore of us, pass out ahead. And before the day was over the old *Cornwall*, with the heartiest lot of lads that ever swung a scoop throwing coal under her boilers, covered a wide stretch of the South Atlantic at a speed a good knot or two better than she had averaged on her trial trip, or at any other time since then.

"There was one trivial but amusing little incident in connexion with the departure of the battle cruisers which stands out particularly clearly among my otherwise rather jumbled memories of those two hours of rush and hurry. We had been leading our usual hand-to-mouth existence in the matter of food for some weeks previous to this, and one of the things we had most looked forward to our call at Port Stanley for was revictualling. We were losing no time in getting provisions aboard, and at the moment the signal to raise steam was received a lighter containing, among other things, a large cask of beer and a lot of salt pork had just moored alongside. We were really in great need of the salt pork, and—well, there seemed to be a considerable desire for the beer also. However, when the Devil drives, or a reckoning is to be settled with the Hun, one can't wait for such incidentals as food and drink. Knowing that we had enough aboard to keep going on until the game was played out, I ordered the lighter to cast off and turned my attention to more pertinent matters. I recalled later that I heard the winch grinding once or twice after I gave the order, but, seeing the lighter floating away with the tide presently, thought no more about it for the moment.

"Carried hither and thither by the conflicting harbour currents, the lighter was half a cable's length or so off our port bow when the battle cruisers, spouting smoke like young volcanoes, came charging out to take up the chase of the Hun, and, by a strange chance, it was lounging indolently square athwart the course of the Flagship. The sharp bows of the *Invincible* shore it through like a knife, and her propellers, with those of the *Inflexible*, quickly reduced boat and cargo to bobbing bits dancing in their bubbling wake.[A]

"It really hurt me to see that good food and drink snatched almost out of our mouths, as it were, but I tried to put on a brave front and turn the matter off as a joke. 'Beer and pork sausage,' I remarked to one of my officers who had just come up to the bridge to report; 'the battle cruisers seem to have a good appetite for Hun diet this morning. I only hope they'll have as good luck gulping down the Huns themselves.'

"'It's only "sausage" they put their teeth in, I'm glad to say, sir,' he replied with a grin. 'The men managed to hoist the beer aboard somehow before casting off the lighter, and as I came along just now I heard some one ordering that the cask be put down in a "syfe plyce wher' it won't be 'oled if th' 'Un 'its us."'

"'My word!' said the Captain, with the same look on his face that it had worn on another occasion when he had told me of the 'banquets' that had been served on the *Carmania* when the *Cornwall* had foregathered with her at a certain mid-Atlantic rendezvous after the former had sunk the *Cap Trafalgar*. 'My word! but we *did* enjoy that beer when the time came to drink it. Yes, they shared and shared alike with the officers. Good old pirate law as to loot and salvage, you know.'

"The *Kent*, which was at five minutes' notice, was the first ship to get under weigh, probably with orders to keep the enemy in sight but not, of course, to try to engage them. The *Glasgow* was the next out, and then the *Carnarvon*. The *Cornwall* was ready to follow close on the heels of the latter, but, as I have told you, had to wait for the battle cruisers, which were now under weigh. We went out not far astern of the *Inflexible*, and the *Bristol*, which had been on long notice in the inner harbour, was last, at a considerable interval.

"The battle cruisers, with their turbines, worked up to full speed a great deal more rapidly than the ships with reciprocating engines, and, heading straight down the wake of the retreating Germans—now showing their fore-shortened silhouettes in 'Line Ahead' on the south-western horizon—they quickly drew away from all but the *Glasgow*. The latter, not long out of the dry dock and swiftest of the lot in any event, had passed the *Kent* and was holding a southerly course, evidently with the intention of keeping the Hun light cruisers in sight and reporting their movements.

"It took something like two hours after the British ships were out to convince Von Spee that all his efforts to go 'mehr schnell' were going to be of no avail. There was nothing left for him to do but to 'der fight gemachen.' In this he had two alternatives—to fight with all of his ships, or to fight a delaying action with a part of them and give the others a chance to escape. His choice was the one that any other sailor as gallant and able as Von Spee had proved himself to be would inevitably have taken. He plumped to fight with the *Scharnhorst* and *Gneisenau*, and let the *Nürnberg*, *Leipzig*, and *Dresden* make the most of their chances of scattering to safety. His signal, as we learned it later from prisoners, was substantially this: 'Light cruisers will make every endeavour to escape to South American ports. Armoured cruisers will engage enemy, and endeavour to delay.'

"It was just about noon that I saw the tower-like, smoke-crowned silhouettes of the German ships gradually begin to lengthen, and when they held steady more or less beam-on I knew that the turn of eight points meant that Von Spee had made his decision. As the dark profiles began to draw apart—the two longest heading to port and the three shortest to starboard—I realised at once what that decision was. The armoured cruisers were going to try to draw the pursuit to the south, while the light cruisers sought safety by 'starring' on divergent courses to the south and south-west.

"I think there will be no harm in my telling you that in all the possible contingencies we had discussed under which we might meet the enemy, there was none which roughly approximated to the conditions imposed upon us by the fact that he had unexpectedly come upon us in harbour—

surprising us no less than himself—and forcing us to tumble out in pursuit of him in much the same order as a farmer and his family sallying forth following an alarm in their hen roost. What we had generally agreed would happen was that we—ourselves spread over a wide expanse of sea in 'Line Abreast'—would sight the enemy steaming in similar formation, and in that event it was understood that our battle cruisers should attend to the two German armoured cruisers, while the rest of us took on such of his light cruisers as we could most readily bring to action. Though already scattered over many miles of sea, our problem was really only that of conforming this 'elastic' general plan to present conditions.

"The battle cruisers altered course instantly to continue the chase of the enemy armoured cruisers, but the Admiral, doubtless realising that, scattered as we were, each of the rest of us (already conversant with his general instructions) would be his own best judge as to where he could be most useful, left us to pick our own quarries. I made up my mind at once to go after the light cruisers, and, signalling 'Come on, *Kent*' (the Captain of the *Kent* was my junior, and therefore subject to my orders in a case of this kind), headed off in the direction of what were still little more than three dark blurs on the south-westerly horizon. The *Glasgow*, which was a long way ahead to port, also decided (in view of instructions) in favour of going after the light cruisers, and, altering course sharply, passed astern of the battle cruisers and converged with the *Kent* and *Cornwall* in the chase. The *Carnarvon*, which for some reason was not steaming her best, and had been left a good distance astern, held on after the battle cruisers. The *Bristol*, which had been delayed in getting out of harbour, had been ordered to look after some steamers which had been following Von Spee, and which we believed to carry coal and provisions. We afterwards learned that one of them had a cargo of potatoes, and as potatoes chanced to be another of the many things which the *Cornwall* was short of at this time, I have always harboured the same kind of grudge against the *Bristol* for sinking these as I have against the *Invincible* for putting down my salt pork.

"As soon as it became evident what courses the Hun ships were steering, I signalled to the *Kent* to go after the port ship, which turned out to be the *Nürnberg*, while I gave my attention to the middle one of the three, the *Leipzig*. This would have left the *Glasgow* free to pursue and engage the third ship, the *Dresden*, which her twenty-six knots of speed should have enabled her to do handily. This plan, if it could have been carried out, would have made a clean sweep of Von Spee's squadron then and there, instead of giving the *Dresden* a new lease on life, and some weeks more of uncertainty for merchant vessels of both the South Atlantic and Pacific. Where it slipped up was through the fact that the *Glasgow* could not avoid engaging the *Leipzig en passant* while endeavouring to get within range of the *Dresden*, and, once having taken on the latter, she was, bulldog-like, reluctant to draw off until her opponent was finished. As there was no other ship fast enough to catch up the *Dresden*, her escape was inevitable.

"It was a little after four in the afternoon—almost to a minute the time I had reckoned it would be—that the fine burst of speed the *Cornwall* had been putting on brought the *Leipzig* well within range, and I gave the order to open fire. Previous to this the latter had been engaging in a very lively little running fight with the *Glasgow*, neither appearing to be inflicting serious damage to the other. The Hun's four-point-ones were about balanced by the *Glasgow's* equal number of four-inch, but the latter's two six-inch gave her a comfortable margin that would have decided the issue in her favour in the end. The German gunners, always at their best at the beginning of an action, were making good practice, however, and the *Glasgow* would have known she had had a fight on her hands before it was over.

"At the intervention of the *Cornwall*, with her fourteen six-inch guns, the *Leipzig*—very pluckily and properly—turned her attention to the heavier armed, and therefore the more dangerous, of her two adversaries. We began hitting her at our third salvo, and it must have been about the same time that a shell from one of her well-served four-point-ones came crashing into the *Cornwall*. I must say it was jolly good work for such comparatively small guns. The extremely high angle they had to be fired at, though, reduced their chances of hitting, and I recall especially one beautifully bunched salvo which struck the water so close to the far side of the ship that it might almost have been dropped from an air-ship.

"One of the gunners told me an amusing incident in connexion with that first hit. A boy, engaged in passing six-inch shells, was inclined to be rather nervous at the outset, and was coming in for a good deal of chaffing from his more callous mates. When the bang and jar of that first explosion ran through the ship, a shell had just been handed him to shove along, but, quivering all over, he stood rooted in his tracks and demanded to know what the noise was. A guffaw of laughter ran round, at the end of which an old gunner replied, 'That, me son, is our fust vaxinashun mark.' Gradually a grin of comprehension and reassurance replaced the look of terror on the lad's face as he realised that it isn't necessarily so serious a thing after all to have a shell burst above your head. 'Right-o!' he cried, passing the shell smartly on; "and this proj. on to the 'Un an' prevent a small-pox epidemic breakin' out 'board *'is* ship.' The joke had passed all the way round the ship before the fight was over, and there was red-hot rivalry to the end to keep the Hun's small-pox rate down by 'vaxinashun.' When you think of it, there's nothing funny about the joke at all; but there's nothing equal to the roughest of chaff to keep men's spirits up and their nerves steady in a fight, and it's because these lads of ours take fighting in the same happy-go-lucky spirit that they take their sport that they're such incomparable stayers—that they're always going stronger at the finish than when they started, no matter what the course.

"I remember another amusing little incident which occurred at about this stage of the game. Owing to the fact that there was no voice-pipe connexion from the bridge to the foretop and other 'nerve-centres,' it was imperative that I should fight the ship from the conning tower—an irksome necessity on account of the circumscribed vision. I found myself making occasional rounds of 'afternoon calls' to the various places with which I wanted to keep in closer touch, or from where I had a better chance to see how things were progressing than from the box of the conning tower, and one of these took me to the bridge, whose sole occupant was the signalman at the range-finder. Silhouetted black against the sky and with not enough cover to protect him from a pea-shooter, he was still going quietly about his work and apparently having the time of his young life.

"The *Liepzig's* gunnery had not begun to go to pieces at this juncture, and every little while one of those beautifully bunched little salvoes of four-point-ones would throw up its pretty nest of foam jets in the near-by water. A shell from one of these struck somewhere amidships as I came out upon the bridge, and I found the man at the range-finder just throwing an appraising glance over his shoulder to where the fragments of a whaler were mounting skyward in a cloud of smoke. 'My word, sir,' he greeted me with, 'but it's jolly glad I am I ain't back ther' w'ere the projers catch you 'tween decks. Now, up 'ere it's diff'rent—they just passes straight on into the water.'

"'They pass straight through!' I repeated. 'What do you mean by that?' 'Jest wot I sez, sir,' he replied. 'Look w'ere you're standin', sir! The canvas ain't 'arf stiff enuf to stop 'em.'

"I looked. On my left the canvas wind-shield was punctured with a smooth round hole at about the level of my waist, while on my right a similar strip had been pinked about even with the calf of my leg. From the upper hole the ragged ends of the painted canvas were bent inwards: from the lower hole, outwards.

"'Twas from the 'Uns' last salvo but one, sir,' said the signalman, grinning down at me over the range-finder. "Twould 'a' jest about plugged you in the knees. You was jest too late in comin' up, sir.'

"I believe I told him," said the Captain with a laugh, "that, while I should hate to be setting an example for unpunctuality on my own ship, I sincerely hoped and trusted that I should continue being equally late for 'appointments' of that kind. He was a brave chap, that one, and I'm glad to say my recommendation brought him a D.C.M. for the way he carried on that afternoon.

"It's very funny the things one 'imagines' in the course of an action, one in which you are being hit, I mean. There isn't a lot of your ship that you can see from a conning-tower, and so when anything happens—like the explosion of a shell, for instance—you (generally more or less subconsciously, for your whole active mind is engrossed with fighting the ship) have to speculate on where it struck and what damage it did. Here is an example of one of my efforts in this line that afternoon. A terrific smashing-banging followed the explosion of a shell somewhere amidships, and from the nature of the racket I instantly jumped to the conclusion that it could be only one thing. 'After funnel carried away,' I announced to my Staff Paymaster, whom I had kept standing by to take notes and the time of any incidents I thought worth recording, though just why I concluded it was the *after* one I don't remember. 'After funnel carried away,' he repeated, and jotted down the entry against the time the disaster had occurred.

"Well, I carried on for the next hour or two with the distinct idea in my mind that one of the funnels was gone, and I even recall wondering several times in the course of the next hour or two whether any damage had been caused in the engine-room, or whether the wreckage was likely to get afire, or whether the smoke would be getting in the way of the guns. Indeed, it is quite possible I tried to get some assurance on these points by voice-pipe. I don't remember precisely. At any rate, it was quite definitely fixed in my mind that that funnel was gone, so that when the next time I poked out to have a look round, I found that it was not even dented, I could hardly believe my eyes. I really am not quite sure to this day what it was that made the infernal banging which I took to be that funnel going over the side.

"Everything considered, the *Leipzig* made as gallant a fight as it is possible to conceive. Under the fire of two ships, either of which was faster and more heavily gunned than herself, knowing all the time that her sister ships—almost as completely outclassed as herself—could never be counted upon to come to her aid, and, finally, desperately short of ammunition, the way in which she carried on to the end was worthy of the traditions of any navy. Indeed, it has often occurred to me that Von Spee and his officers—from their long service on the China station—had kept themselves entirely free of the contaminating influences of Potsdam which have made the names of the High Sea and the U-boat fleet words anathema. British Naval Officers who had met those of the *Scharnhorst* and *Gneisenau* in the Orient still speak of them with kindness, and even occasionally with affection, and certainly no one could have faced defeat and death with a finer or more resolute spirit than they did at the Falklands. Perhaps, for the sake of their souls, it was fortunate that they never got nearer home than the South Atlantic.

"As I have told you, it was about our third salvo which made our first hit upon the *Leipzig*, a shell of this carrying away her topmast. The latter, in falling, appears to have killed the Gunnery Lieutenant, which must inevitably have made it at least a temporary interference with the control. The Torpedo Lieutenant, whom we picked up among the survivors, took over the direction of the firing from the foretop from that time on.

"There was no appreciable falling off in the *Leipzig's* firing until the fight had been in progress about two hours. Then the hammering from our shells began to tell rapidly, and at about six-thirty, when I noted that both her mainmast and after funnel had been carried away, and that she was blazing with heavy fires in several places—the firing became spasmodic, and finally, with the exception of a single gun, ceased altogether. At this juncture, as I learned subsequently, there were but eighteen unwounded men left in the ship, and it was a 'scratch' crew of these who, bringing up odd shells from wherever they could find them, continued the fight as long as they had anything to fire. Then they lit their pipes, sat down on the deck and waited for the end.

"At seven-fifteen, seeing her engines had failed her and that she was lying an apparently helpless hulk in the trough of the now rising sea, I gave the order to cease firing. Scarcely had I done so, however, when there came another flash from that one unsilenced gun, and its well-placed shell pierced the paint-room in the *Cornwall's* forepeak. The ensuing clouds of smoke were so dense that I gave orders for the fire to be extinguished with all despatch. Luckily, the fumes proved to have come almost entirely from the shell itself. It was only afterwards, of course, that I learned in what desperate straits the *Leipzig* was at this moment. At the time, as she still appeared desirous of carrying on the fight, I had no choice but to commence firing again. This last salvo or two was quite thrown away, however, that is, so far as settling the fate of the enemy was concerned. Indeed, the injury done to her in the first two hours of the fighting would ultimately have sent her to the bottom, while the fact that her shells—except for the odd ones chivvied together for the one gun—must have been at an end about the same time would have left her quite incapable of doing us much harm save with a torpedo. As I have said, however, I did not know these things then, and so could only continue trying to inflict the heaviest damage possible as long as she kept firing.

"That shot through my paint-lockers was the last fired by the *Leipzig*, and I have good reason to believe that the shell was literally the last four-point-one left on the ship. Two or three of Von Spee's ships had wasted a good bit of their quite irreplaceable munitions in what must have been an almost useless bombardment of Papeete, in the French Societies, while on their way across the Pacific, and Coronel made still further inroads into the magazines. I do not know whether any other ship, like the *Leipzig*, exhausted all its heavy shells before being sunk, but all of them must have been very low in any case. This fact fully vindicates the decision (which I told you of some time ago) resolved upon by those responsible for the disposition of the greatly inferior force of British ships in South American waters before the intention of sending out the battle cruisers was known, to seek out and fight Von Spee, regardless of the odds, in the hope of clipping his claws for the future by compelling him to fire away as many as possible of his remaining shells.

"As soon as it became evident that the *Leipzig* was incapable of further resistance, the *Glasgow* (as the senior ship) signalled 'Do you surrender?' but to this there was no reply. Whether this failure to respond was fortuitous or deliberately intentional I was never able to learn definitely, but, from the fact that her flag was kept flying to the last, I am inclined to the belief that it was the latter. It is still possible, however, that she had no halyards, flags, lights, or anything else to signal with, even had she so desired. She *did* send up a Verey light at this juncture, but whether that was intended to convey some message to us, in lieu of any other means of doing so, or whether it was a sort of gesture of farewell to any of her sisters that might still be afloat, we never knew. If the latter, it failed of its purpose, for the *Dresden*, the only one of Von Spee's ships still above water, had melted into the mists of the horizon hours before.

"On the chance that the rocket was meant as a distress signal, we steamed in as close as seemed wise, considering the fact that even a sinking ship may launch a torpedo most effectively, and lowered away our boats with all despatch. The fact that, with a seven per cent. list to port due to being holed twice below the water-line on that side, it was difficult to lower the boats to starboard, as well as the fact that several of our port boats had been smashed by shellfire, hampered the work of relief, and the *Leipzig* had gone down, while the nearest whaler was still some distance away. Any of the wounded that may have got clear of the sinking ship succumbed quickly to the icy coldness of the water, but of the eighteen unwounded men remaining after the action closed, sixteen were picked up—eleven by the boats of the *Glasgow*, and five by those of the *Cornwall*.

"One burly Hun, picked up by my coxswain whom I had sent in charge of my galley, gave the lad the surprise of his life, when he exclaimed (in impeccable Cockney English), the instant he was safe aboard: 'G'blyme, myte, but ein't it bally cold?' I found out later that he had been for a number of years an interpreter in the Law Courts of Sydney, Australia. An extremely significant admission that he made me in the burst of confidence induced by thankfulness at finding himself safe and sound after the hell he had been through, was to the effect that he had received notice of mobilisation toward the end of June. One could not ask for better evidence than that of the deliberation with which Germany prepared for the war which she has made such frantic efforts to delude the world into thinking was 'forced' upon her by the Allies—in August!

"My greatest surprise of the day, and certainly the most welcome, came when I asked for a report on our casualties. There were none, or rather only one—the ship's canary, killed in its cage when a shell exploded in the wardroom pantry. This, considering the fact that the *Cornwall* had been hit eighteen times by four-point-one shell, was indeed good luck, and fully vindicated the plan I had followed of fighting the earlier stages of the battle at a range which, while short enough to allow my heavier guns to do deadly execution, was still somewhat extreme for the lighter ones of the enemy. The latter, it is true, were sighted up to a very considerable range, but both their accuracy and effectiveness fell off greatly as the angle at which they had to be elevated to carry these long distances was increased.

"The battle cruisers had opened fire on the enemy armoured cruisers somewhere about noon. As it was not for an hour or two after that time that our divergent courses had taken us out of sight of each other, we had a good view of the early stages of the action. Here again the Huns opened with their usual spectacularity, and I think I am correct in saying that I saw one of their eight-point-twos crash home on the *Invincible* before either of them had been struck by a twelve-inch shell from the battle cruisers. The balance was redressed a few minutes later, and long before the action became to us four lines of flame-splashed smoke on the distant horizon, it was plain that the Huns were already beaten. The *Scharnhorst*, Von Spee's Flagship, which had come in for rather more than her share of the fire up to that time, went down with her flag flying at about four o'clock. The *Gneisenau* kept up a brave but unequal fight for two hours longer, which gave the *Carnarvon* time to come up and help administer the *coup de grâce*.

"Until our closing up on the *Leipzig* made it necessary to call the men to action stations, those who were free to do so had swarmed over the ship in search of the best points of vantage from which to watch the fight between the heavy cruisers. They couldn't have cheered with more enthusiasm if it had been a football game and the flame-shot smoke-spurts when the battle cruisers' shells exploded on the Huns were goals for the ship's team. They went down eagerly enough when 'Action Stations!' sounded, but it was because I knew that, even in the heat of their own fight, they must be wondering how that other one was progressing that I had the word passed round to them when, about six-thirty, the wireless brought the stirring news that the battle cruisers had finished their work and the *Scharnhorst* and *Gneisenau* were no more. Well—it was a great moment when the *Leipzig* went down an hour later, but I am not sure that even that sight stirred me more deeply than did those muffled but still ringing cheers that came welling up to my ears from those brave lads, sweating in their stuffy 'tween decks stations, when they heard of the success of the *Invincible* and *Inflexible*.

"When the last of the survivors of the *Leipzig* had been picked up in the gathering darkness, we put the old *Cornwall* about and headed back to Port Stanley. Short of coal, and with a heavy list to port where the *Leipzig's* shells had let water into the bunkers, ten knots was about as fast as I cared to steam her. That, and a thick fog for a part of the time, was responsible for the fact that we were twenty-four hours in returning a distance we had negotiated, with all our zigzaging, in less then ten on the way to the fight. The day following our arrival I found 'rest and change' in a wild-goose hunt in the marshes not far from Port Stanley."

FOOTNOTES:

[A] Admiral Sturdee has since assured me that he distinctly recalls seeing his Flagship cut down a drifting lighter as he put to sea in pursuit of Von Spee.

THE STORY OF THE *SYDNEY*

I. THE SIGNALMAN'S TALE

It may be that it is because, since the outbreak of the war, the British sailor has constantly been riding the crest of the wave of great events, that he is so prone to regard even the most dramatic and historic actions in which he has chanced to figure as little or nothing removed from the ordinary run of his existence, as only a slightly different screening of the regular grist of the mill of his daily service. Thus, I once heard a young officer describing a night destroyer action in which he had played a notable part as having been "like a hot game of rugger, only not quite so dirty," and another assert that his most vivid recollection of a day in which he had performed a deed of personal daring that had carried his name to the end of the civilised world was of how "jolly good" his dinner tasted that night.

It was this attitude which was largely responsible for the fact that, although there were upwards of the three or four score officers and men who had taken part in the sinking of the *Emden* still in her, I spent several days in the *Sydney* before I found any one who appeared to consider that stirring action as anything other than the mustiest of ancient history, and, as such, of no conceivable interest at a time when every thought was centred upon the vital present and the pregnant future rather than upon the irrevocably buried past. And in the end it was more by luck than deliberate design that the two actors in the historic drama which I had set myself the task of learning something of at the first hand came to tell me of the parts they had played. That they were the two who had had what were perhaps more comprehensive opportunities for observation than any others was my sheer good fortune.

It was toward midnight of a day of light-cruiser "exercises" that I first stumbled upon the trail which I had hitherto sought vainly to uncover. With all hands at "Night Defence" stations and steaming at half speed through the almost impenetrable blackness, we were groping blindly for an uncertainly located target in an endeavour to reproduce the conditions under which enemy destroyers might be expected to be encountered in the darkness. Suddenly the sharp bang of a small calibre gun sounded, followed by the shriek of a speeding projectile, and presently the glare of a down-floating star-shell shed its golden-grey radiance over the misty surface of the sea. Instantly the unleashed searchlight beams leapt to a distant little patch of rectangular canvas gliding along through the luminous fog on our port beam, and the fraction of a second later—following the red flame-stabs and the thunderous crashes of a broadside—it disappeared in the midst of ghostly green-white geysers of tossing spray. It was while—flash-blinded and gun-deafened—I fumbled about on the deck of the signal bridge for the "ear-defender" that the nervous jerk of my head had flirted loose, that I heard a quiet voice speaking in the darkness beside me as a hard hand brushed mine in the search.

"You'll find, sir, that cotton wool's a good sight better than one of them patent ear protectors," it said. "I suppose it was one of them 'Mallet-Armours' that you plug in. I had a pair of that kind when we went after the *Emden*, and they kicked out just like yours did at the first salvo. You can bet I was deaf as a toad before we finished polishing her off.

"I was watching the whole of that show, sir, from just where you're standing now," the voice went on after the lost "defender" had been found and replaced, "and it was just behind you that the shell that sheared off our range-finder and killed the range-taker passed on through the screen and into the sea. It was either that shell or the fragment of another (I could never quite make sure which) that cut off and carried away one half of a pair of prism glasses hanging there, leaving the other just as good as ever. We still have the remnant in our mess as a memento."

Flash and roar and that spectral upheaving of foam-fountains in the converging rays of the searchlights crowded most other things out of the next hour or two, and it was only when the night-firing was over and we were headed back for our anchorage in the cold light of the early dawn that I discovered that it was a young signalman who had been standing watch beside me during the exercises. Keen and alert he looked in spite of the sleepless night behind him, and it was easy to believe him when he told me that his had been the honour of being the first man in the *Sydney* to sight the "strange ship" which subsequently turned out to be the long-sought-for *Emden*.

"It was just the luck of my chancing to be on watch with a good pair of glasses," he said modestly; "but that was by no means the limit of my luck in connexion with the *Emden* show. When we went to 'Action Stations,' I was ordered to come up here and do nothing but keep an eye on the collier that had been standing-by the *Emden* at first, but which got away under full steam just as soon as it was plain we were going to give her 'whats for.' I carried out orders all right as far as keeping an eye on the collier was concerned, but my other eye, and my mind, were on the *Emden* ring of the circus. I don't really suppose there was another man on the *Sydney* who had as little to do, and therefore as much time to see what was going on, as I did. But that wasn't the end of my luck, for I was one of the party that went ashore the next morning to round up the Huns that had landed on Direction Island, and then, after that, I was in the first boat that went to bring off prisoners from the *Emden*. So you see I had a fairly good-all-round kind of a 'look see.' My training as a signalman made it natural for me to jot down things as I saw them, and I think that I still have a page of memorandum where I made notes during the fight of what time some of the things happened. If you'd like to see it, sir——"

Then I knew that I at last had the sort of story I had been looking for in prospect, and before going below for my cup of ship's cocoa as a preliminary to turning in I had arranged for a yarn in the first Dog Watch that evening. It was indeed good luck to hear the account of the historic action from one who, besides having had such exceptional opportunities for seeing the various phases of it, also appeared to be well educated and a trained observer.

"I'm sorry I couldn't find one of the *Emden's* cat-o'-nine-tails," were my visitor's first words when he appeared at the door of the Captain's sea-cabin where I awaited him after tea; "but the fact is that the most of us have taken the best of our little remembrances of that show ashore for safe-keeping, and those 'dusters' were the things we prized more than anything else as showing the Hun up for the bully he really is.

"What did they use them for? Well, if you'd believe their story, it was to dust their togs after coaling ship. We brought back about twenty of them, with the rest of the salvage, and at first we were rather inclined to take it for straight when they said they used them for dusters. Then one of our prisoners got hold of more than his share of our beer one night, and became drunk and truthful at the same time. He confessed that they had been used on the men time and time again, just in ordinary routine, to keep them up to the mark on discipline. He also said that they had been used freely during the fight with the *Sydney*, and that when the lashes failed to give sufficient 'encouragement,' something more drastic was used. But I'll tell you about that in its place. But you see what real prizes those 'cats' were, sir, in the way of holding the Hun up to the light so you could see through him, so to speak. *My* 'cat' was a brand new one, but the most of the lot were black and stiff with blood.

"We'd been rather playing at war up to the time we fought the *Emden*," he went on, "having spent most of the opening months purifying the Marshalls, Carolines, New Britain, and New Guinea by cleaning the Huns out of them. There had been a few skirmishes ashore, but nothing at all at sea, nor did the prospects of anything of the kind seem any better in early November than they had been right along up to then. We missed our big fight when, with the *Australia*, *Melbourne*, and the French cruiser, *Montcalm*, we came within twenty-four hours of connecting with Von Spee's squadron when they swept through the South Pacific on their way to South American waters. With that gone, there didn't seem much to look forward to until we were sent to the North Sea, and we were rather hoping, when we set out from Australia with a convoy in the first week of November, that we might keep going right on to Europe.

"We knew, of course, that the *Emden* was still in business, but we also knew that any one ship had about as much chance of finding her in the Indian Ocean as you have of finding the finger-ring you lose in the coal bunkers. Certainly we didn't expect that going out in force with a convoy would be the means of bringing her to the end of her tether.

"The first and only word we had that a raider was in our vicinity was in the form of a broken message from the Cocos station, which never got further than 'Strange cruiser is at entrance of harbour———.' At that point the 'strange cruiser' managed to work an effective 'jam,' and it was not long before the Cocos call ceased entirely. Although we did not learn it till a couple of days later, this was caused by the destruction of the station by a landing party from the *Emden* under Lieut. Mucke.

"The escorting warships were the *Sydney*, her sister, the *Melbourne*, and a Japanese cruiser, larger and with bigger guns, but slower than we. The Jap, without waiting for orders from the Captain of the *Melbourne*, who was the senior officer of the convoy, dashed off at once, and was only recalled with difficulty. A message which the Japanese captain sent to account for his break was most amusing, 'We do not trust the skipper ship *Emden*,' it read, 'he is one tricky fellow, and must be watched.'

"As the job was one for a fast light cruiser, the choice was between the *Sydney* and *Melbourne*, and it was because the skipper of the *Melbourne*, who was the senior officer, did not feel that he had authority to leave the convoy that the *Sydney* had the call. We worked up to top speed quickly, and were soon tearing through the water headed for Cocos Island at over twenty-six knots an hour.

"I don't remember that there was any especial excitement in the *Sydney* that morning. We had dashed off on too many wild-goose chases already to feel that there was very much of a chance of finding our bird this time. In fact, I don't remember being as nervous at any stage of this *Emden* show as in a night attack we made upon Rabaul, in New Britain, where never a shot was fired. There had been some 'Telefunken' messages in the air during the night (undecipherable, of course), but that was only to be expected. Every one seemed even more inclined to crack jokes than usual, and that is saying a good deal. I remember especially that some of the officers were making very merry over the fact that Lieut. G—— prepared for action by going to the barber and having his hair cut, something that he didn't do very often.

"It was about seven in the morning when the broken message was picked up, and at eight I was sent aloft to relieve the lookout. It was nine-fifteen when the ragged fringe of the cocoa-nut palms of Direction Island—the main one of the Cocos-Keeling group—began to poke up over the horizon, and perhaps ten minutes later that my glasses made out the dim but unmistakable outline of three funnel tops.

"Although we hadn't studied silhouettes at that stage of the game to anything like as much as we've had a chance to since, that trio of smokestacks marked her for a Hun, and probably the *Emden* or *Königsberg*. Just which it was we never knew for certain till after we'd put her out of action and picked up the crew of the collier that accompanied her.

"Just before I went aloft I heard one of the officers make an offer of a pound to the Boy that was first to sight the enemy. I didn't come under that rating myself, but it occurred to me instantly that it would never do to let all that money go unearned. So I leaned over, broke the news to a pukka Boy who was aloft with me, and told him to sing it out. He got the quid all right, and, for a long time at least, he got all credit and kudos of actually being the first to sight the *Emden*. When I finally told the Captain about the way it really happened, he laughed and said it served me right for trying to dabble in 'high finance.' I never understood quite what he meant, but always fancied 'high' had some reference to me being aloft, and 'finance' referred to the quid.

"The first sign of life I saw on the *Emden* was when she started blowing her syren. This, although we did not know it at the time, was an attempt to call back the party she had sent ashore to destroy the wireless station. Luckily for that lot there was no time for them to come off. The *Emden* did not, as I have read in several accounts of the action, attempt to close immediately, but rather headed off in what appeared to be an endeavour to clear the land and make a run of it to the south'ard. It was only when her skipper saw that the converging course we were steering was going to cut him off in that direction that he took the bull by the horns and tried to shorten the range to one at which his four-point-ones would have the most effect.

"There is no use denying that we were taken very much by surprise when the enemy fired his ranging shot at 10,500 yards, for we had hardly expected him to open at over seven or eight thousand. Still more surprising was the accuracy of that shot, for it fell short only by about a hundred yards, and went wobbling overhead in a wild ricochet.

"His next was a broadside salvo which straddled us, and his third—about ten minutes after his 'opener'—was a hit. And a right smart hit it was, too, though its results were by no means so bad as they might have been. I had the finest kind of a chance to see everything that that first shell did to us. It began by cutting off a pair of signal halyards on the engaged side, then tore a leg off the range-taker, then sheared off the stand supporting the range-finder itself, went through the hammocks lining the inside of the upper bridge, and finally down through the canvas screen of the signal bridge (behind where you were standing last night) and on into the sea. If it had exploded it could hardly have failed to kill the Captain, Navigator, and Gunnery Lieutenant, and probably pretty well all the rest of us on both bridges.

"You may well believe, sir, that we were rather in a mess for some minutes following that smash, but I remember that the officers—and especially the Captain and Navigator—were as cool as ice through it all. The Captain went right on walking round the compass, taking his sights and giving his orders, while the 'Pilot' was squatting on top of the conning tower and following the *Emden* through his glasses, just as though she had been a horse-race. I even remember him finding time to laugh at me when I ducked as one or two of the first shells screamed over. 'No use trying to get under the screen, Seabrooke,' he said; 'that canvas won't stop 'em.'

"It was almost immediately after this that the after-control—located about amidships—met with even a worse disaster through being hit squarely with two or three shells from a closely bunched salvo. I had a clear view in that direction from where I stood, and chanced to be looking that way when the crash came. I saw a lot of arms and legs mixed up in the flying wreckage, but the sight I shall never forget was a whole body turning slowly in the air, like a dummy in a kinema picture of an explosion. As the profile of the face showed sharp against the sky for an instant, I recognised it as that of a chap who had been rather a pal of mine, and so knew that poor old M—— had 'got his' a couple of hours before I heard it from the Surgeon.

"It was some minutes before there was any chance to look after the range-taker whose leg had been taken off by that first shell. They bundled the mangled fragments of his body together as best they could in one of those Neil Robertson folding stretchers, and I helped the party get it down the ladders. As the leg was cut off close up to the body the poor chap had bled terribly, and there was no chance of saving him.

"While I was edging along the deck with the stretcher-party, I saw, out of the corner of my eye, what appeared to be a very funny sight—one of the gun crew of 'S2,' which was not engaged at the time, dabbling his foot in a bucket of water. When I came back I saw that it was anything but funny.

"Two of the crews of starboard guns had been badly knocked about by the explosion of shells striking the deck at the end of their long high-angle flight. Among these was the chap I had seen apparently cooling his feet in a water-bucket. As a matter of fact, it was no foot at all he was dabbling, but only a maimed stump. The foot had been carried away by a shell fragment, and the brave chap, not wanting to be put on the shelf by going down to the Surgeon, had—all on his own—scooped up a canvas bucket full of salt water and was soaking his stump in it in an endeavour to stop the flow of blood. He was biting through his lip with the smart of the brine on the raw flesh as I came up, but as I turned and looked back from the ladder leading up to the bridge I saw him hobble painfully across the deck and climb back into his sight-setter's seat behind his gun. I have forgotten now whether it was another wound, or further loss of blood from this one, which finally bowled him over and put him out of the fight he wanted so much to see through to a finish.

"These I have mentioned were the several shots from the *Emden* which were responsible for our total casualties of four killed and eleven wounded. Of other hits, one took a big bite out of the mainmast, but not quite enough to bring it down. Another scooped a neat hollow out of the shield of the foremost starboard gun and bounced off into the sea, leaving two or three of the crew who had been in close contact with the shield half paralysed for a few moments from the sharp shock.

"Still another ploughed through a grating, two bulkheads and the Commander's cabin, and finally nipped into the sea, all without exploding. Next to the knocking out of the range-finders, perhaps our most troublesome injury was from a shell-hole in the fo'c'sle deck, through which the water from the big bow wave the *Sydney* was throwing up entered and flooded the Boys' Mess deck. By means of the water-tight doors we managed to confine the flooding to that flat only.

"There is no doubt that for the first fifteen or twenty minutes of the fight the *Emden* had the best of it. This was probably due mainly to her luck in putting both our range-finders out of action in what were practically her opening shots.

"It took her three ranging shots to find us, though, and, once we started, we did the same with her. Our first salvo fell beyond her, the next both short and wide, but two or three shells from the third found their mark. And we were no less lucky than the *Emden* with our first hits, for where she knocked out our gunnery control by disabling our range-finders, we did the same to her by shooting away the voice-pipes of her conning tower, from which Captain Von Müller directed the action.

"Just as soon as we started hitting the *Emden* she stopped hitting us. In fact, I don't think from then on to the end she dropped another shell aboard us. Going aft to see if a small cordite fire had been put out, I noticed the crew of one of the port guns—'p. 3,' I think it was, which was not in a position to train at that moment—amusing themselves by chalking messages on their shells. I don't remember all of them, as there was a good deal of a variety. One shell had 'Emden' on it, to make sure it would go to the right 'address,' I suppose. Another had 'Cheerio' and 'Good Luck' on it, and another simply 'Kaiser.' They were a proper lot of 'don't-give-a-hangs,' that crew.

"With the *Emden's* shell no longer bursting about our ears, I had a better chance to watch the effect of our fire upon her. I still have the page of memorandum on which I noted the time that a few things happened during the next hour. I will run through it so you can see just the way the show went. At ten o'clock the range was about 8000 yards, a distance which the Captain evidently reckoned our guns would do the most harm to the *Emden*, and hers the least to us. She was trying to close this for some time, but the *Sydney* was using her superior speed to keep her right there, so that, in a way, she was chasing us at this stage of the game.

"The effect of our fire upon the *Emden* first began to show just after ten, and at 10.4 I made a note that her fore funnel had disappeared. At 10.30 our lyddite caused a big explosion at the foot of her mainmast, making a fire which never was entirely got under control. At 10.34 her foremast, and with it the fore-control, collapsed under a hard hit and disappeared over the far side. At 10.41 a heavy salvo struck her amidships, sending the second funnel after the first, and starting a fierce fire in the engine-room. At 11.8 the third funnel went the way of the other two, and when I looked up from writing that down I saw that the fore-bridge had done the disappearing act.

"Almost immediately the *Emden* altered course and headed straight for the beach of North Keeling Island, which she had been rapidly nearing during the last hour. The *Sydney* fired her last salvo at 11.15, and then, the Captain seeing that the enemy was securely aground, turned away and started in hot pursuit of the collier.

"This collier, as we learned presently, was a former British ship, the *Buresk*, which had been captured by the *Emden* some time before and put in charge of a German prize crew. If her skipper had not felt sure that the *Emden* was going to do for us, he could have easily steamed out of sight while the engagement was on. As it was, he lingered too long, and we had little difficulty in pulling up to a range from which we could put a warning shell across the runaway's bows. That brought her up, but the Hun naval ensign was kept flying until a signal was made for it to be struck. That brought the rag down on the run, but her skipper prevented it falling into our hands by burning it.

"No sooner was our boarding officer over her side than a mob of Chinese stokers crowded about him shouting in 'pidgin' English that 'puff-puff boat gottee biggee holee. No more top-side can walkee.' Rushing below, our men found the sea-cocks open, with their spindles bent in a way to make closing impossible. As the ship was already getting a list on, there was nothing to do but take the prisoners off and let her go down.

"To make sure that there was no trick about the game—that no concealed crew had been left behind to stop the leaks by some prearranged contrivances and steam away with her as soon as it was dark—the *Sydney* pumped four shells into her at short range, and she was burning fiercely from fires started by these when the water closed over her. Then, at a somewhat more leisurely gait, we steamed back to see how it fared with the *Emden*.

"It was now about the middle of the afternoon, and the first thing we noticed—standing out sharp in the rays of the slanting sun—was the naval ensign flying at the still upright mainmast of the *Emden*.

"The instant he saw this, the Captain made the signal, by flag, 'Do you surrender?' To this *Emden* made back, by Morse flag, 'Have no signal books,' which meant, of course (if it was true), that she couldn't read our first signal. Then, using Morse flag, which they had already shown they understood, we repeated the signal, 'Do you surrender?' There was no answer to this, and again we repeated it. As there was still no answer, and as there was no sign whatever of anything in the way of a white flag being shown anywhere, the Captain had no alternative but to continue the action. I have always been glad that I heard the Captain's orders to the Gunnery Lieutenant at this time, for the point is one on which the Hun survivors were even then ready to start lying.

"We were at fairly close range, and I heard Lieut. Rahilly ask the Captain upon what part of the ship he should direct his fire. The Captain studied the *Emden* through his glass for a few moments and then, remarking that most of the men appeared to be bunched at opposite ends of the ship—on the fo'c'sle and quarterdeck—said he thought that there would be less chance of killing any one if the fire was directed somewhere between those two points. Then I heard him give the definite order, 'Open fire, and aim for foot of mainmast,' and that was the word that was passed on to the guns.

"The port guns fired (if I remember right) three quick salvoes, and we were just turning to give the starboard ones a chance, when a man was seen clambering up the solitary stick of the *Emden*, and the word was passed, 'Don't fire without further orders.' At the same time a white flag, which I later learned was a tablecloth, was displayed from the quarterdeck. A moment later the naval ensign fluttered down, and shortly I saw the smoke of new fire on the quarterdeck. I surmised rightly that they were following the example of the *Buresk* in burning their flag to prevent its capture, but what else was going up in that fire I did not learn until I swarmed up to that deck the next day.

"It was an unfortunate fact that our guns, which there had been no time to overhaul, were suffering a good deal from the strain of their hard firing during the battle. As a consequence their shooting was by no means as accurate as at the beginning of the action, and several of the shells went wide of the point at which it was endeavoured to direct them.

"There is no doubt that they wrought sad havoc among the crowd on the fo'c'sle, and I don't think our prisoners were exaggerating much when they said that those three last salvoes killed sixty and wounded a good many more, and also that a number of others were drowned by jumping into the surf in the panic that followed. One could feel a lot worse about it, though, if the whole thing hadn't been due to the sheer pig-headedness of their skipper in trying to bluff us into letting him keep his flag up. He has the blood of every man that was killed by those last unnecessary shots on his hands, just as much as his brother Huns have those of the women and children they have murdered in France and Belgium.

"Von Müller was brave all right. There's nothing against him on that score. But it was nothing but his pride and a selfish desire to keep his face with his superiors whenever he got back to Germany that led him to force us to fire those entirely needless shots into his ship. He thought that he would cut a better figure at his court-martial if his colours were shot down rather than lowered in surrender. But if he was so anxious to make a proper naval finish, why did he run his ship ashore instead of fighting it out on the seas the Huns make such a shouting about battling for the freedom of? If he had done that instead of trying to bluff us like the bully the Hun always is, he'd have saved a good many lives that he sacrificed in trying to save his own name. There would have been a few wounded drowned in that case that were saved by beaching the *Emden*, but these were more than offset by his forcing us to fire those last shots that there was no need in the world for firing if Von Müller hadn't tried to bluff about the flag.

"I've never had any patience, sir, with all that has been said and written about Von Müller being a sportsman. That reputation was gained wholly through the sportsmanship of the *Sydney's* officers who, because they'd given the *Emden* a licking in a fair give-and-take fight, didn't think it was quite the proper thing to speak ill of her captain, even if it was the truth.

"And one other thing, sir, while I'm speaking of this incident. Every time I hear any one talk about negotiating with the Huns I tell them, that story of Von Müller's bluff about his flag. He pretended not to understand our signals just because it served his purpose not to understand them. But when our guns began to talk he had no difficulty in translating *their* language. Well, sir, the Huns are all alike. They never will understand any language but that of guns until their bully streak is knocked out of them with guns. It's a dirty job, sir, but that's the only way to finish it."

The lad's fine blue eyes were flashing, and his face red with excitement, and he took out a handkerchief and wiped the perspiration from his brow before resuming his narrative.

"It was getting too late in the day to start rescue work on the *Emden*," he went on more quietly, "and so we did the best we could for her for the present by sending in a boat, manned by prisoners from the *Buresk*, with food and water, and a message to the effect that we would return early in the morning. Then we put out to sea, for we thought we still had to reckon with the *Königsberg* turning up at any moment, and didn't want her to surprise us as we had surprised the *Emden*.

"Crossing the track of the battle, we sighted and picked up three Hun seamen, who claimed to have been blown from the deck of the *Emden* by the explosion of one of our shells, none of them much the worse for their experience. Indeed, the fact that they were not in worse shape rather led us to suspect that they had jumped overboard to *avoid* the explosion of our shell rather than as a direct consequence of an explosion.

"I don't exactly remember whether it was one of these chaps, or one of the English-speaking prisoners from the *Buresk*, who, by blurting out something about how lucky were his mates who got ashore before the fight started, gave us our first inkling that the *Emden* had sent a landing party to Direction Island to destroy the Wireless station. There were three officers and forty men, he told us, and this we later learned to be the truth.

"What he did not tell us—quite possibly because he did not know of it—was the fact that, besides being armed with rifles, this party also carried three machine guns. It was only by chance that our failure to reckon with this latter fact did not get us into serious trouble. Indeed, I think it is more than likely that I would not be here talking to you now but for the happy fact that the little schooner *Ayesha* lying in Direction Harbour offered a chance of escape too promising for the officer in command of the party to resist.

"The rounding up of this lot, of course, had the call over everything else, and at first the Captain appeared to be considering putting back to Direction at once and landing in the night. Lucky, indeed, it was for us that we didn't, for that—as we learned later from the Wireless-station people—was just what the Germans had expected and prepared for. Had we gone in in the night we would have found the only landing-place covered by machine guns, and we would probably have stepped off into an ambush that would have wiped the lot of us out in a minute or two. Landing at dawn, however, we found our birds flown, and I, for one, was jolly glad to hear it after they had told us what a resolute fellow the German officer leading the party was, and how determined he had been to make a resistance. This chap, by the way, was Lieut. Mucke, who later found his way back to Germany by way of Turkey. When I read, three or four months later, of how well he had used those same machine guns he had mounted to receive us against the Arabs in fighting his way up the coast of the Red Sea, I realised the extent to which we had been asking for trouble in landing armed only as we were. Not expecting any resistance, we had no machine guns, and I think there were several others who, like myself, had been given only revolvers. Since the *Sydney's* lucky star was in the ascendant for the whole show, however, no harm came of it.

"You may be sure that the Wireless-station people were glad to see us, for they had never been sure until they had seen the last of Mucke and his men just how the Huns might use them in case the latter determined to fight it out to the last ditch on Direction Island. One of them told me that he had visions of being used as a human shield against the *Sydney's* shells, like the Huns used the women and children in Belgium. They were a proper devil-may-care lot, those ones, and I can quite believe the story that they asked the Huns to come and play tennis with them when they got tired of watching the one-sided fight between the *Sydney* and *Emden*.

"As we were in a hurry to get back to the *Emden*, we did not remain long ashore on Direction. Their doctor came off with us to help with the wounded, and with him came two or three others of the Wireless people to have a hurried 'look-see' at the *Sydney*. These latter intended to return to shore at once in their own boat, but, by some mistake, the whaler was cast off and the *Sydney* got under weigh while the Inspector was still in conversation with the Captain. They were about to ring down to stop the engines, when the chap, with a good-bye wave of his hand, ran to the port rail and disappeared in a header over the side. A moment later he reappeared, settled his helmet back upon his head, and struck out in a leisurely way for the boat which was pulling back to meet him. It was quite the coolest thing of the kind I ever saw, but I didn't appreciate it fully until an hour or so later when I saw the black triangular fins of countless 'tiger' sharks converging from every direction upon where the *Emden* had been casting her dead into the surf of North Keeling Island.

"Scarcely had we entered again the waters through which the battle had been fought than we began to sight floating bodies. This was only to be expected, of course, but what did surprise us was to come upon a wounded man, in a lifebelt, being pushed slowly shoreward by an unwounded mate who had nothing whatever to keep him up. Although they had been in the water all of twenty-four hours, both were in fairly good shape when we picked them up, and the unwounded chap was quite his own Hunnish self again after he had had a night's sleep and a couple of square meals. In fact, if I remember right, he was one of the worst of several of the prisoners who seemed to think it was their privilege to keep the stewards told off to look after them running day and night after 'bier.'

"As we neared the *Emden* I saw that she was flying the International signal for 'In want of immediate assistance.' We lowered two boats, and in the one of these under Lieut. G—— I was sent along in case there was any signalling to be done. It was a nasty job getting aboard her, for she was lying partly inside the surf and the swells were running high even under her stern. As she was at right angles to the seas, there was no lee side to get under, and so we had to do the best we could boarding her as she was. Lieut. G—— had a hard scramble for it, and only the hands extended him by a couple of the German officers saved him from a ducking. Watching our chances, the rest of us swarmed up between swells, but it was touch-and-go all the time and took a long while.

"Frightful as the wreck of the *Emden* looked from the sea, it was nothing to the sheer horror of it as you saw it aboard her. The picture of it is still as clear in my memory as if photographed there. I will tell you first about the ship itself. The great and growing hole in her bows, where she was pounding the reef, could be seen by leaning over the side. Of the fore-bridge, only the deck remained. The chart-house was gone completely. The foremast, though more or less intact to the fore-top, had been shattered at the base by shells, and was lying over the port side, shrouded with wreckage.

"The fore-control top I could not find at all, and the fore-topmast had also disappeared completely. From the foremast to the main, which was still standing, was one tangled mass of wreckage, and of this the Wireless room, which looked like a curio shop struck by lightning, was the worst mess. Two of the funnels were knocked flat over the port battery, crushing several bodies under them, and a third—the foremost one—was leaning against the wreck of the bridge. All about the starboard battery the deck was torn with gaping holes, and through these one could see that the whole inside of her was no more than a blown-out and burnt-out shell. There was one place where it was a straight drop from the quarterdeck to the inner skin of the bottom.

"But it was the men—the dead and wounded—that provided the real horror. In the first place, there had been something over 350 officers and men in the *Emden*. When we boarded her, 185 of these were alive, but something like half of them were wounded, most of them very badly. This number included a score or so who had jumped or been blown overboard, and had swum, waded, or been washed by the surf on to the beach of the island. Even the unwounded were very cowed and apathetic, the only exceptions I remember being the Captain and one or two other officers. By no means all of the dead had been thrown over in the twenty-four hours that had now passed since the battle, and not nearly as much had been done for the wounded as might have been done, even considering the difficulties. Some of the wounded had not even been dragged out of the sun, and it was the wounds of these (as I learned later from one of our sick bay stewards) that were much the worst infested with the maggots, which the tropical heat had started breeding almost immediately because no antiseptics had been applied. A considerable quantity of medical stores had been uninjured by the fighting, I was told, and the proper use of these would have made the greatest difference in saving lives and preventing a lot of suffering. I could tell you just what swine it was that was responsible for this, but I'd rather you got the facts from one of the officers. I think our Surgeon could tell you something of the way things were.

"Horrible as were some of the mutilations from shell fragments, by far the most shocking injuries seemed to have been inflicted by our lyddite. The hair and clothes were entirely burnt from some of the bodies, and the sides of these which had been exposed to the blast of the flame-spurts were cooked to the colour of cold mutton. Most of the bodies that had been thrown or blown overboard were being washed in to the beach by the surf, and there was a fringe of them lying in rumpled heaps above high-water mark. This was only about a hundred yards from the bow of the *Emden*, and some of our men said that they saw the big land-crabs crawling and fighting over them, and also worrying some of the wounded who had crawled a little further inshore under the coco palms. These men ashore had most of them jumped overboard when those three last salvoes were pumped into her, and as it was not possible for us to reach and bring them off till the following day, their sufferings from thirst and from the attacks of the crabs must have been very terrible indeed. All of this would, of course, have been avoided but for Von Müller's trying to bluff us into leaving his flag flying after his ship was beached and out of action.

"Most of the unwounded men who jumped overboard were probably washed ashore before the sharks had a chance to get to them, but the more helpless of the wounded who went over outside of where the surf was breaking must have been attacked almost at once. The sea tigers were still fighting over some of the fragments even after rescue work had commenced, and I still shudder when I think of the shock it gave me the first time I saw a floating body start to wriggle as a shark nosed into it from beneath. It was a seaman in a white suit and sun-helmet, floating face down, and as the monster seized it, the jerks made it give two or three quick overhead flops of the arms, for all the world like a man striking out to swim the 'Australian Crawl.' There were sharks following along astern of every boat-load of wounded we pulled back to the *Sydney*, just as if they thought we were robbing them of something that belonged to them by rights.

"But perhaps the thing that shocked me most of all, terrible as were the sights on every hand, was something one of the surviving officers (I think he was of 'Warrant' rank) said to me shortly after I came over the side. Although he was quite unwounded, he was lolling in the shade of a blanket thrown over some wreckage, and making no effort to help in the thousand and one things that might have been done to ease the sufferings of his mates. He spoke fairly good English, and I learned afterwards he had been a steward on a 'Nordeutscher Lloyd' liner on the Australian run. Raising himself on his elbow, but not leaving his comfortable retreat, he called out to me, 'I say, my poy, vy vos it der *Zydny* ev'ry time turn to us stern on 'stead of bows on?' There was the Hun for you. That little point about the way the *Sydney* happened to turn once or twice had evidently puzzled him, and the question had been occupying his Hunnish mind at a moment when any other kind of a human being but a German would have been working his head off to make life a little less of a hell for the men who had fought beside him and under him. Sickened by the shambles all round, and half-choked as I was by the horrible reek from the bodies of the dead and wounded, it took all the control I had to keep from putting my foot in the ruffian's bloated face.

"I learned a good many things in those few hours I spent in the *Emden* of the way of the Hun officers with their men, and the 'cat-o'-nine-tails' I have told you of were not the worst.

"A rather decent sort of chap, who said that he had learned his English working on a Scotchman's farm in Argentina, took me to a doorway leading to a flat from which a ladder had descended to the engine-room and stokeholds. Across that doorway was lying the body of an officer, which nobody seemed to have taken the trouble to move. He was the Gunnery Lieutenant, the chap said, and had been driving up stokers at the point of his revolver to serve a gun whose crew had been knocked out when he was killed. The officer's body was somewhat scorched by lyddite, but from the line of the burns it looked as if they were made after he fell.

"What looked to me very much like a bullet wound in the side of the head struck me at once as the likely cause of his death. 'Did one of his own men shoot him?' I asked; but the chap—seeing a young officer who, I later learned, was Prince Franz Joseph Hohenzollern, a relative of the Kaiser, approaching—only shrugged his shoulder and raised his eyebrows and walked away. I didn't like to ask about the incident after the men were prisoners on the *Sydney*, but just the same there has never been any doubt in my mind as to what occurred.

"Most of my time on the *Emden* was put in standing by on the quarterdeck in case there was any signalling to be done, and this gave me a good chance to get a line on a little ceremony which had been carried out there just after she sent her flag down.

"We had seen them burn that flag, but just what other things went into that fire we never knew exactly. The nature of some of them, however, I began to surmise when I came upon charred fragments of Bank of England notes lying about among the wreckage and sticking in the cracks of the warped deck. Several coins which I picked up turned out to be English shillings and German marks. I noticed that some of our lads were pushing the search with much energy whenever they had a chance, paying especial attention to the cracks between the charred planking and the deck. When fire-blackened gold sovereigns began to make their appearance in the *Sydney*, and kept appearing even after we had been for months in the West Indies and South Atlantic, I understood the reason for their energy.

"When the prisoners were searched on board the *Sydney* several of them were found to be in possession of English sovereigns (one of them gave the Paymaster a bag containing over a hundred for safe keeping), which they claimed to be their own. It was not until they had been disembarked at Colombo that it turned out that one of them had confessed that among other things thrown into that fire on the quarterdeck of the *Emden* was all the treasure she had seized from the British merchant ships she had sunk during her career as a raider. This included sixty thousand pounds in gold sovereigns and an unknown amount in bank notes. The latter were consumed, and the gold, after the bags had been burned away from it, was swept into the sea. It was in this way that the few stray coins picked up lingered behind in the gaping cracks opened up by shells bursting in the enclosed spaces under the quarterdeck."

At this juncture a messenger came to summon my young friend to the signal bridge, but he lingered at the door long enough to say that he had fully made up his mind to go back to North Keeling Island after the war and have a try at raking up some of that scuttled treasure.

"There's no sand where she was lying, sir; only hard coral reef that ought to catch the coins in the holes and prevent them from being washed away. My only fear is that the coral may grow over and cover it up before I am free to get out there. Do you know how fast a coral island grows, sir?"

I replied that I was not sure about it, but that I seemed to have some kind of an impression that the coral insect couldn't erect much more than a thirty-second of an inch of island a year, adding that I didn't think that a few inches of coral could make much difference with a big heap of gold like that in any case.

"Perhaps not, sir," he assented; "but all the same I'm hoping that it won't have had time to grow even *one* inch before the war's over. The stuff's no use to a chap unless he can have it while he's young."

II. NAVAL HUNNISM
SOME INSIDE HISTORY FROM THE FALKLAND AND COCOS ISLAND BATTLES

Perhaps there is nothing about which the German has been more contemptuous of the Briton than in the matter of the way the latter has of treating war as he does his sport, of fighting his battles in the same spirit with which he plays his games. Yet it has been this very desire of the latter to play the game at all stages that is responsible for the fact that the German, for a time at least, was given credit in the popular mind of even the neutral and Allied countries for a great deal that never should have been credited to him. This is especially true of two or three of the earlier naval actions of the war. The fact that a German captain fought his ship gallantly seemed to his British opponent of that period sufficient reason for forgetting, or at least forgiving, him for not fighting fairly, and so it was that the bravery of Von Spee at the Falkland, and the skill and pluck of Von Müller in the *Emden* at Cocos Island, had the effect of mitigating in the minds of the officers of the British ships, which emerged as victors from those battles, the impression of a number of things, ranging all the way from "not playing the game" to downright treachery. And so it chances that in the eyes of even the civilised world the Germans have been given a clean sheet for these earlier encounters, and one hears them spoken of to-day in London as though they stood apart in this respect from every battle the German has fought on sea—or on land for that matter—since then. It is regrettable to record that this popular belief has no more to base itself on than the sportsmanlike reticence of the British officer in refusing to broadcast the real facts. One had a sort of pleasure, as the record of the Hun grew blacker and blacker the more chance he had to give expression to his real self, in hugging that delusion that the sailors of the *Scharnhorst* and *Gneisenau* and *Emden* were at worst only a dull grey in comparison with their infamous mates of the High Sea Fleet who were drawn upon to man the U-boats. But that they were all of a kind one has only to talk with any of the British officers and men who came in contact with them in and after battle to learn beyond dispute. I will cite a single instance from the Falklands before going on to the *Emden*, on which latter even more false sentiment has been wasted on the score of the supposed "sporting" behaviour of her officers than on any other of the German ships which were in the limelight of publicity during the opening months of the war.

After the *Scharnhorst* and *Gneisenau* had been sunk off the Falklands by the *Invincible* and *Inflexible*, the latter ships made every possible effort to pick up all the Germans who had survived the fighting and were floating in the water. A considerable number of these were brought aboard Admiral Sturdee's Flagship, the *Invincible*. Among the few German shells which had struck the latter battle cruiser was an "eight-point-one" which had failed to explode. Knowing that Von Spee had been near the end of his munition, but wishing to gain indisputable evidence on that point by establishing beyond a doubt whether the shell in question contained an explosive charge or was only a practice projectile fired for want of anything better, Admiral Sturdee decided to have it taken to pieces. Thinking it might be useful to get the testimony of the prisoners on the matter first, the Admiral, after having the shell in question brought to his cabin, ordered that the captured Germans be sent in for interrogation. Without exception they all declared that the projectile before them was made only for practice, and that, as it carried no explosive charge, there would be no risks whatever in knocking it apart to prove that fact. Questioned specifically as to whether any special precautions need be taken in handling it, they replied with equal unanimity in the negative.

As the prisoners began to file out, however, one of them caught the Admiral's eye and shook his head slightly, as though to convey—without his mates observing it—a warning that the shell was dangerous. On calling this man back, the Admiral was informed that the projectile really contained a full charge of high explosive, and that tinkering with it before certain precautions were observed would inevitably result in detonating it. A keen student of human nature, Admiral Sturdee recognised at once the unparalleled opportunity to test German honour and study a phase of the then imperfectly understood German psychology. The prisoners were ordered to be brought in separately, and in such a manner that those who passed out after interrogation should have no chance to communicate with their mates who were waiting their turn. To each man as he appeared it was pointed out that he owed his life to the fact that the British had not followed (as they well might have) the precedent set by the Germans at Coronel of making no effort to pick up the survivors from the ships they had sunk. It was also pointed out to him that his failure to tell the truth would probably be attended with serious loss of life among those to whom he owed his own. Then the question respecting the nature of the shell was again put. Without a single exception (the man who had confessed was not, of course, examined again) they reiterated most emphatically their former statements that the shell contained no explosive and might therefore be disassembled with impunity.

After providing adequate safeguards, the shell was taken to pieces, and at once proved to be everything that all but one of the several score of rescued Huns had declared it was not, which meant, of course, that if it had been handled in the way these had insisted would be perfectly safe, all near it would have been killed. Since there is no punishment provided for this brand of treachery, no action was taken against the prisoners, and the incident was remembered principally for the illuminative sidelight it threw on the unexpected moral obliquity of the German sailor. It was something quite new in the annals of civilised naval warfare, and Sturdee's officers were scarcely less grieved than shocked that men who had fought so bravely could behave so despicably. Yet that (to the Germans) incomprehensible sporting code of the British, by which it reckoned as not "playing the game" to speak ill of a brave foe after he is beaten, has prevented the story from finding its way to the public, and it is only now, when four years more of war have established the fact that the action of the Huns on this occasion was characteristic rather than (as so many of Sturdee's officers tried so hard to persuade themselves at the time) exceptional, that I am given permission (by one who observed at first hand all that took place) to publish it.

Perhaps (doubtless on account of the greater spectacularity of the lone-hand game she played) the *Emden* and her able and resourceful Captain came in for more of this misplaced credit than any other of the German cruisers of similar career. In one instance this even went so far as to prompt the people of the sporting Australian city from which the ship which brought the *Emden's* career to a finish took her name to request that the doughty Von Müller and his surviving officers should be sent to Sydney that they might be tendered a public reception. This kindly but misdirected instance of sportsmanship on the part of a people who—at this stage of the war at least—saw nothing incongruous in treating an enemy who had put up a good fight in precisely similar a way to which they had been accustomed to treat a visiting cricket eleven, was occasioned largely by the fact that the officers of the *Sydney*, in their eagerness to do full justice to a beaten foe, laid stress in their accounts of the fight on his bravery and said little or nothing of anything else. Yet, when one comes to learn the real facts of this historic battle (as I have done recently, by talking at length with a number of the British officers and men who took part in it), he finds evidences of "Hunnisms" splashing with muddy spots a record which might have been golden bright on the score of physical courage and devotion to duty.

It is no pleasure to write what I have to set down here, for I am quite frank to confess that the story of the *Emden*, according to the first accounts that were published of it, in connexion with the classic exploit of Lieutenant Mucke in escaping from Cocos Island in a small sloop and ultimately reaching Constantinople by way of Arabia, stirred my imagination as few episodes of the war have done. The time is long past, however, when the German has a right to expect anything further in the way of chivalrous reticence in the recording of his deeds and misdeeds. What I am setting down here was told me by an officer of the *Sydney* who boarded the beached *Emden*, and was also entrusted with the task of rounding up and bringing off the men from the latter that had jumped overboard and made their way to the beach of North Keeling Island.

As regards the battle itself, no one in the *Sydney* has anything but admiration for the pluck and skill with which the *Emden* fought a losing battle against a faster and more heavily gunned ship. But perhaps the one thing which they do hold most heavily against Von Müller personally is for the characteristically Prussian way he tried to bluff them, after he had run his ship aground, into allowing him to leave his flag flying when the *Emden* had been put completely out of action and was out of the running for good and all. I have already written of this historic incident in considerable detail as it appeared to a signalman of the *Sydney* who had unusually favourable opportunity for observing just what transpired, so that it will suffice here merely to summarise it and record that this man's version is fully borne out by what was subsequently told me by officers.

When the *Sydney* returned to the grounded *Emden* after pursuing and sinking the latter's collier, it was seen that the German Naval ensign was still flying at her maintopmast. Nothing in the nature of a white flag was displayed anywhere upon her. After making three times the signal, "Do you surrender?" and each time receiving only an evasive reply, or none at all, the Captain of the *Sydney* had reluctantly to give the order to reopen fire. The three broadsides which were required to convince Von Müller that his bluff would not go down are estimated to have killed sixty men in the *Emden* and to have caused a number of others to jump over into the surf. These lives were nothing more or less than a sacrifice on the altar of Von Müller's Prussian pride, and under the circumstances he was just as blood-guilty for causing them to be snuffed out in a typically Hunnish attempt to "put one over" on the ship that had beaten him and make the report of his defeat read better in Potsdam as if he had ordered them to be mown down by the guns of the *Emden*.

Lieutenant X——'s account of the work he had charge of in the *Emden* shows Von Müller in a better light, but reveal a terrible callousness and negligence on the part of his medical officers. As he must always be the most weighty witness as to how things were on the stricken ship at this juncture, I shall set down his account of what he saw and did in some detail.

"It was the morning after the fight before we had cleaned up all the other incidental business and were free to give our attention to looking after what was left of, or rather who was left in, the *Emden*. Fortunately, her stern was lying out beyond where the surf broke, so that, with a line they threw us from the deck, it was possible to ride under one quarter, with the boat's bow to seaward. I had rather a hard time getting aboard, once nearly falling into the water through getting a hawser between my legs, but I finally managed it through a hand which one of the German officers standing aft reached down to me. I told Von Müller that the Captain of the *Sydney* was prepared to take the surviving officers and men to Colombo provided they would give their parole. At first he rather stuck over the word, as though he would like to make out that he did not understand it, a perfectly absurd bluff in the light of the fact that he was fluent in both English and French, and that the term is in common use by the Germans themselves. He quickly came round, however, when I hastened to explain exactly what the Captain would require of him. Ultimately he signed a paper agreeing that for such time as all officers and men of the *Emden* remained in the *Sydney* they would cause no interference with ship or fittings, and would be amenable to the ship's discipline. This parole was substantially observed.

"The surgeon of the *Emden*, though unwounded, was doing nothing at the time of our arrival, and, from the appearance of the wounded, it was evident that he had done very little during the twenty-four hours which had elapsed since the action. By way of excuse, he claimed that his staff were all killed and his dressings and instruments destroyed. Accepting this as the literal truth, we made a signal for more medical supplies to supplement those already brought, and Dr. Ollerhead, the Eastern Extension Telegraph Company's surgeon, who had come with us from Cocos Island, set to work to get the wounded ready to be transferred. Neither at that time, nor during the three days in which the surgeon of the *Sydney* worked without rest to save as many as possible of the *Emden's* eighty wounded, did the German surgeon render anything like the assistance that might have been expected from him under the circumstances.

"What disgusted us most, however, was to find before we left the *Emden* that there *had* been ample supplies of uninjured dressings all the time. The action station of Dr. L———, the surgeon in question, had been in the stokehold, which was quite undamaged. A bent and twisted ladder or two formed the only obstacles to reaching and utilising the considerable stores of dressings, lotions, etc., which were still available there. Although it was true that the assistant surgeon was missing (he had come on deck after his station in the tiller flat aft had been struck, and was blown overboard by an exploding shell), it was *not* true by a long way that there was not ample help, skilled and unskilled, available for at least first-aid dressing all around, and on this they had hardly made a beginning."

A brief quotation or two from the report of the surgeon of the *Sydney* may be interesting while on the question of the neglect of the *Emden's* wounded by their own surgeon. Referring to the wounded which had just been brought aboard, he says:

> "In cases where large vessels of the leg or arm had been opened, we found torniquets of pieces of spun yarn, or a handkerchief, or piece of cloth bound around the limb above the injury. In some cases, I believe the majority, they had been put on by the patients themselves. One man told me he had put one on his arm himself. They were all in severe pain from the constriction, and in all cases where amputation was required, the presence of these torniquets made it necessary to amputate much higher than one would otherwise have done. *There was little evidence of any skilled treatment before they arrived aboard.*"

Again he writes:

> "Some of the men who were brought off to the *Sydney* presented horrible sights, and by this time the wounds were practically all foul and stinking, and maggots 1/4 inch long were crawling over them, only 24 to 30 hours after injury. *Practically nothing had been done to the wounded*

sailors, and they were roughly attended to by our party and despatched to us as quickly as possible."

Professional etiquette evidently operated to restrain the surgeon of the *Sydney* from stating in his report what he thought of these very palpable evidences of neglect on the part of his "opposite number" in the *Emden*. When I met him in the *Sydney* last winter I heard him express himself in no uncertain language on the subject, but I do not feel at liberty to quote him without his permission, and he has recently returned to Australia. I take it that he reckoned that to his medical brethren, to whom his report was especially addressed, the plain statements of the facts were sufficient to speak for themselves.

Lieutenant X—— credits the German officers with doing the best they could in helping him transfer the wounded. "Shortly after I came over the side," he said, "I took the opportunity to tell Von Müller that we reckoned he had fought very well. To this he merely answered with a rather surly 'No,' and turned away as though to hide his chagrin. Presently, however, he came up to where I was standing, and, speaking in a rather apologetic tone, said: 'Thank you very much for saying that, but I was not satisfied. We should have done better. You were very lucky in shooting away all my voice-pipes at the beginning.' I do not remember whether or not I told him that this was hardly enough to balance his own luck in getting both our range-finders in the first five minutes.

"The best of the whole lot of officers, however—indeed, the only one who showed anything like the spirit one would expect a British officer to display under similar circumstances—was Lieutenant ——, whom I encountered in connexion with my 'sweep' of North Keeling Island after the lot of Huns who landed there through the surf. I was a good deal puzzled to account for the sporting spirit of —— on this occasion—until he chanced to tell me that his mother was English! I had this little Keeling Island roundup all to myself, and, grim as some features of it were, it had also its amusing side, and you may be interested in hearing something of it.

"When we fired those last three broadsides into the *Emden* a good many men either jumped or were blown into the water, and of these a score or more were carried to the beach by the surf. Most of these, as I found later, were wounded in one way or another, and having no food or water, their sufferings during the day and a half before help reached them were unspeakable.

"From the *Emden* the bodies of men—some of which appeared to have life in them—were visible on the beach above high-water mark, and just before we left the wreck for good I noticed a party setting off along the shore to the right. If I had only *failed* to notice this move, my rescue party would have reached the poor wretches eight or ten hours earlier than it did, and probably have saved several more lives than we saved. The unfortunate delay was also largely due to my ignorance of the fact that North Keeling Island was a coral atoll.

"When we got back to the *Sydney* with the last of the wounded from the *Emden* I learned that our galley had already been sent away to take food and water to the men on the beach, but that, for some reason, it had gone in no further than the line of the outer reef where the surf began to break. I volunteered to go in the whaler to find what the trouble was, and if possible, make a landing with both boats. Just as I was about to go over the side, a young Australian lad—some kind of a Boy rating—came and asked to be taken along. I refused him rather shortly, as I thought it would be of more hindrance than help in the kind of job we had on hand. He disappeared quickly, and I did not see him again until we had taken the galley in through the surf and were pulling it up on the beach. Then he was discovered, curled up under the thwarts, where he had managed to stow himself away before we pulled off from the *Sydney*. It was a lucky thing he came along, for, as it turned out, he was the only one of the lot of us who knew how to climb a coconut palm in true native fashion.

"It was impossible to take a boat through the surf anywhere near the point where the *Emden* had grounded, but some miles up the beach there appeared to be an opening in the reef through which a landing might be made. Watching our chances, we managed to shoot the whaler in without an upset, incidentally showing the way to the galley, which had been on the point of giving up the job after staving a hole in its bottom in attempting a passage at a less favourable point. Mustering my men, I set out to find the Huns. It was here that I went wrong.

"Knowing that the island was but a small one, and having seen a number of the *Emden's* men making off to the right from the point where she was grounded, I figured that I would be likely to intercept them more quickly if I circled round to the left and met them face to face than by trying to overtake them. As it was late, I was anxious to lose no time in getting them together and into the boats while there was still daylight to see to getting the latter through the surf. If the island had been anything but a coral atoll my reckoning would have worked out all right; as it was it upset things completely.

"The island was covered with coco palms, under which there was a thick growth of pandanus and some sort of salt grass, the latter forming a tangle which made walking extremely difficult, and ultimately forced me to take to the beach to get opener going. Even here progress was slow on account of the sand and coral clinkers, and it was already getting dark when we suddenly found our way barred by a swift-flowing tidal passage connecting the open sea and what I now saw for the first time—the lagoon in the heart of the coral atoll. The island, like all others of its kind, was in the shape of a rough letter 'C,' with water between the two tips, and therefore quite impossible to walk around.

"As it was out of the question trying to swim what was probably a shark-infested passage in the dark, especially as there was no certainty of finding our men on the other side, there was nothing to do but turn back. Here again I made the mistake of trying to take a short cut by striking straight across the island instead of sticking to the beach. I never saw the place in daylight which we stumbled into, and so can't say just what it was; it seemed, however, to be a sort of wilderness of reeds peopled with a million seabirds, many of them nesting. The roar of our guns in the battle was as nothing to the bedlam of screams which arose when I went slithering through a lot of eggs and flopped full length into a rising mass of beating wings. They came batting against us in the darkness throughout the several minutes we were groping our way back to the open of the beach.

"It was well after midnight when we got back to where the boats were, and so quite out of the question trying to do anything further in the way of searching for the Huns till daylight. Several of the latter had struggled in and given themselves up, and they told us that the rest were all at the point where they had first come ashore from the *Emden*, and suffering greatly from hunger and thirst. As we had expected to be putting back to the *Sydney* within an hour or two of the time we landed, we had little food and water save that in the boats, and this wouldn't have gone very far with the lot of us if it had not been supplemented by the coconuts our young stowaway brought down for us.

"There was not much chance to rest that night on account of the small land-crabs which kept crawling over you the moment you dropped off to sleep, and it was not pleasant to think of how those more or less helpless Huns were faring a few miles farther down the beach. We started off at the first streak of dawn, and reached them by sun-up. The most of them were in even worse condition than I had feared, for it seemed inconceivable to me that they should not have contrived in some way or other to get hold of some coconuts to eat and drink. It turned out that they had not done so, however, and that, as a consequence, a number of them had died of thirst. The worst case, perhaps, was that of the assistant surgeon, whom I told you of as having been wounded and blown overboard by a shell. Delirious from thirst, he had managed to induce a sailor to fetch him a drink of salt water, and had died shortly afterwards as a result of drinking it. All the open wounds, since they had gone from twelve to eighteen hours longer without attention, were in even more terrible condition than those of the men we had found on the *Emden* the previous day.

"The only one of the lot who seemed to have any hold on himself was the Lieutenant ——— I have mentioned. Luckily, he was not injured, and he appeared to have been doing everything he could to help those that were. It must have kept the plucky chap's hands full, for several of them were crazy, and a number of the wounded were too helpless to keep the crabs away. He and one or two of the least knocked out of the seamen had managed to keep these vermin pretty well away from the bodies of the living, but with the dead down along the water's edge they were already having their way.

"Finally, we got all the helpless of the wounded on to stretchers and started on their way to the boats. ——— was the greatest help throughout, but I can't say as much for many of the others of the unwounded, who were very grudging in the way they lent a hand. ——— put up a stiff protest against going off without burying the dead, declaring that he was not going to leave them there for the crabs to eat up. When I pointed out that we had no implements for digging, and that I needed his help in getting the living off, he saw the reason of it and said he would come along. We did the best we could for the dead by covering them with palm leaves and coral clinkers.

"I made a wide circle around before we left, trying to be sure that none of the living was left behind. The Huns were not quite sure of their numbers, so there was no checking up the thing that way. I am quite positive that no living man was left in that immediate vicinity, and ---- felt equally certain that none had strayed away. This must have been just what *did* happen, however, for, many weeks later, we had word from the Telegraph people to the effect that, when they landed on North Keeling Island to bury the dead, one of the crab-picked skeletons they found was in a sitting position against the bole of a palm tree. I've never tried to reconstruct the story of what happened, but it must have been rather awful at the best.

"It was rather a problem, calculating how to get every one off in two small boats, one of which had a hole in the bottom. The whaler would still float right side up, however, and we finally managed it by putting the badly wounded, with a pulling crew, in the *Sydney's* cutter, which was sent to aid us in the morning, and the rest piling into the whaler and sitting in the water. Then a long tow-line was passed to the cutter (long enough to let her get out beyond the breakers before a strain came on it) and she pulled away with the whole procession. ———, in spite of all I could do to induce him to get into the whaler, insisted on swimming out through the breakers and boarding her outside. If he hadn't been starving and thirsting for forty-eight hours I would have put it down as pure swank; as it was, however, I can't believe he was actuated by anything else than a wish to ease off the load on the damaged boat while it was going through the breakers. He was a thoroughly good sport, that ———, and, as I told you, I was a good deal puzzled to account for it until I learned about his being half English.

"We reached the *Sydney* all right, and the whaler was just being hoisted in when I heard the Captain's voice from the bridge asking where Lieutenant X—— was. I looked up just in time to catch him staring down at me with open-eyed amazement. 'Oh, there he is!' he exclaimed, turning away with a grin on his face. That led me, for the first time in twenty-four hours, to take a look at what I could see of myself without a glass. It was my turn to grin—and to blush. Absolutely the sum total of my wardrobe was my shirt and a seaman's straw hat! Nothing else. To ease my feet from boots after standing on the scorching iron decks of the *Emden*, I had shifted to an old pair of dancing pumps when I returned to the *Sydney* and these, in the rush of departure, I had worn ashore. These, and my socks, must have been scoured off among the coral clinkers, and my cap probably went when we stumbled into the sea-birds' roost in the darkness. But where I lost my trousers, and what sailor gave me his hat, I have never been able to make out."

I asked Lieutenant X—— if it was true, as I had heard, that the officers of the victor and vanquished took advantage of the several days they spent together in the *Sydney* before the Germans were disembarked at Colombo to foregather and talk the battle over.

"Except for the two Captains, who were necessarily thrown together a good deal and who drew a chart of the battle between them, emphatically no," he replied. "The wardroom officers held practically no conversation at all with those from the *Emden*. On their part there was shown no inclination to talk, and on our part that fact alone would have been enough to prevent any interchanges of a personal nature. It would have seemed rather like 'rubbing it in' if we had tried to draw them out on a subject that couldn't but be a painful one to them. Some of the men yarned together a bit, I believe, but you may be quite assured that (save for the exception I have mentioned) there was nothing of the kind between the officers. There wasn't a lot in common between us at the best."

II. LIFE IN THE FLEET

A BATTLESHIP AT SEA

The collier had come alongside a little after seven—two hours before daybreak at that time of year—and I awoke in my cabin on the boat deck just abaft the forward turret to the grind of the winches and the steady tramp-tramp of the barrow-pushers on the decks below.

On my way aft to the wardroom for breakfast, I stopped for a moment by a midships hatch, where the commander, grimed to the eyes, stamped his sea-boots and threshed his arms as a substitute for the warming exercise the men were getting behind the shovels and the barrows. He it was who was responsible—partly through systematisation, partly through infusing his own energetic spirit into the men themselves—for the fact that the *Zeus* held the Blue Ribbon, or the Black Ribbon, or whatever one would call the premier honours of the Grand Fleet for speedy coaling. Not unnaturally, therefore, he was a critical man when it came to passing judgment on the shifting of "Number 1 Welsh Steam" from hold to bunkers, and it was not necessarily to be expected that he would echo my enthusiasm when I told him that this was quite the smartest bit of coaling I had ever seen west of Nagasaki, something quite worth standing, shivering tooth to tooth, with a raw north wind, to be a witness of.

"It's fair," he admitted grudgingly, "only fair. A shade over 300 tons an hour, perhaps. 'Twould have seemed good enough before we put up the Grand Fleet record of 408. Trouble is, they haven't anything to put 'em on their mettle this morning. Now, if some other ship had come within fifty or sixty tons of their record this last week, or if we'd had a rush order to get ready to go to sea—then you might have hoped to see coaling that was coaling."

All through my porridge and eggs and bacon the steady tramp of the barrow-men on the forecastle-deck throbbed along the steel plates of the wardroom ceiling, and it must have been about the time I was spreading my marmalade (real marmalade, not the synthetic substitute one comes face to face with ashore these days) that I seemed to sense a quickening of the movement, not through any rush-bang acceleration, but rather through gradually becoming aware of increased force in action, as when the engines of a steamer speed up from "half" to "full." In a few moments an overalled figure, with a face coal-dusted till it looked like the face of the end-man in a minstrel show, lounged in to remark casually behind the day before yesterday morning's paper that we had just gone on "two hours' notice." A half-hour later, as the gouged-out collier edged jerkily away under the impulse of her half-submerged screw, the commander, a gleam of quiet satisfaction in his steady eyes, remarked that "it wasn't such a bad finish, after all," adding that "the men seemed keen to get her out to sea and let the wind blow through her."

The ship's post-coaling clean up—usually as elaborate an affair as a Turkish bath, with rub down and massage—was no more than a douche with "a lick and a promise." Anything more for a warship putting off into the North Sea in midwinter would be about as superfluous as for a man to wash his face and comb his hair before taking a plunge in the surf.

Once that perfunctory wash-down was over, all traces of rush disappeared. What little remained to be done after that—even including getting ready for action—was so ordered and endlessly rehearsed that nothing short of an enemy salvo or a sea heavy enough to carry away something of importance need be productive of a really hurried movement. Just a shade more smoke from the funnels to indicate the firing of furnaces which had been lying cold, and the taking down or in of a few little harbour "comforts" like stove-pipes and gangways, forecasted imminent departure.

The expression regarding the fleet, squadron, or even the single ship ready to sail at a moment's notice is as much of a figure of speech as is the similar one about the army which is going to fight to the last man. A good many moments must inevitably elapse between the time definite orders come to sail and the actual getting under weigh. But the final preparations *can* be reduced to such a routine that the ship receiving them can be got ready to sail with hardly more than a ripple of unusual activity appearing in the ebb and flow of the life of those who man her. No river ferry-boat ever cast off her moorings and paddled out on one of her endlessly repeated shuttlings with less apparent effort than the *Zeus*, when, after gulping some scores of fathoms of Gargantuan anchor chain into her capacious maw, she pivoted easily around in the churning boil of reversed screws, took her place in line, and followed in the wake of the flagship toward the point where a notch in the bare rounded periphery of encircling hills marked the way to the open sea.

Nowhere else in the temperate latitudes is there so strange a meeting and mingling place of airs and waters as at the "Northern Base." The butterfly chases of sunshine and showers even in December and January are suggestive of nothing so much as what a South Pacific Archipelago would be but with fifty or sixty degrees colder temperature. Dancing golden sunmotes were playing spirited cross-tag with slatily sombre cloud-shadows as we nosed out through the mazes of the booms, but with the first stinging slaps of the vicious cross-swells of a turbulent sea, a swirling bank of fog came waltzing over the aimlessly chopping waters, and reared a vaporous wall across our path.

The flagship melted into the milling mists, and dimmed down to an amorphous blur with just enough outline to enable us a sight to correct our position in line. In turn, the towered and pinnacled head-on silhouette of our next astern ship grew soft and shadowy, and where proper perspective would have placed the fourth was a swaying wisp of indeterminate image which might just as well have been an imminently wheeling seagull as a distantly reeling super-dreadnought. The comparison is by no means so ridiculous as it sounds, for only the day before a naval flying-man had told me how he once started to bring his seaplane down on sighting a duck (which was really some hundreds of feet in the air) because he took it for a destroyer, and how, later, he had failed to "straighten out" quickly enough because he thought a trawler was a duck in flight.

The lean grey shadows which slipped ghostily into step with us in the fog-hastened twilight of three o'clock might just as well (had we not known of the rendezvous) have been lurking wolves as protecting sheep-dogs.

"Now that we've picked up our destroyers," said the officer who paced the quarter-deck with me, "we'll be getting on our way. Let's go down to tea."

Smoke, masts, funnels, and wave-washed hulls, the Whistleresque outlines of our swift guardians had blurred to blankness as I looked back from the companion-way, and only a misty golden halo, flashing out and dying down on our port bow, told where the flotilla leader was talking to the flagship.

Tea is no less important a function on a British warship than it is ashore, and nothing short of an action is allowed to interfere with it. Indeed, how the cheerful clink of the teacup was heard in the prelude to the diapason of the guns was revealed to me a few days ago, when the Commander allowed me to read a few personal notes he had written while the light cruiser he was in at the time was returning to port after the Battle of Jutland. "The enemy being in sight," it read, "we prepared for 'Action Stations' and went to tea." A few minutes later, fingers which had crooked on the handles of the teacups were adjusting the nice instruments of precision that laid the guns for what was destined to prove the greatest naval battle in history.

Tea was about as usual with us that day, save that the officers who came in at the change of watch were dressed for business—those from the bridge and conning-tower in oilskins or "lammy" coats and sea-boots, and the engineers in greasy overalls. A few words of "shop"—steam pressure, revolutions, speed, force and direction of the wind, and the like—passed in an undertone between men sitting next each other, but never became general. The sponginess of the new "potato" bread and the excellence of the margarine came in for comment, and some one spoke of having rushed off a letter just before sailing, ordering a recently advertised "self hair-cutter." A discussion as to just how this remarkable contrivance worked followed, the consensus of opinion being that it must be on the safety-razor principle, but that it couldn't possibly be worth the guinea charged. All that I recall having been said of what might be taking us to sea was when an officer likely to know volunteered that we would possibly be in sight of land in the morning, and some speculation arose as to whether it would be Norway or Jutland. A recently joined R.N.V.R. provoked smiles when he suggested Heligoland.

The cabin which I had been occupying in harbour was one located immediately under the conning-tower, and used by the navigating officer when the ship was at sea, the arrangement being that I was to go aft and live in his regular cabin while we were outside. Going forward, after tea, I threw together a few things for my servant to carry back to my temporary quarters. Groping aft in Stygian blackness along the windward side of the ship, I encountered spray in clouds driving across even the lofty fo'c'sle deck. The wind appeared to have shaken off its flukiness as we cleared the headlands, and, blowing with a swinging kick behind it, was rolling up a sea to match. I did not need to be told by the sea-booted sailor whom I bumped on a ladder that it wasn't "goin' t' be no nite fer lam's," to know that there was something lively in the weather line in pickle, probably to be uncorked before morning.

The grate, robbed of its chimney, was cold and empty when I went in for seven o'clock dinner—half an hour earlier than in harbour—and there was just the suggestion of chill in the close air of the wardroom. An engineer-lieutenant who started to reminisce about a winter cruise he had once made in the Arctic was peremptorily hushed up with a request to "talk about something warmer." A yarn about chasing the *Königsberg* in the lagoons of East Africa was more kindly received, and an R.N.R.'s account of how his ship carried Moslem pilgrims from Singapore to Jeddah on their way to Mecca brought a genial glow of warmth with it. There was something strangely cheering in his story of how, when there was a following simoon blowing across the brassy surface of the Red Sea, the Lascar stokers used to go mad with the heat and jump overboard in their delirium. The air seemed less dank and chill after that recital. I ventured a "sudorific" contribution by telling of the way they made "desert storms" in the California movies with the aid of buckets of sand and a "wind machine." The whole table showed interest in this—probably because it was so far removed from "shop"—and sat long over port and coffee planning a "blower" that would discharge both wind and sand—in sufficient quantities to give the "desert storm" illusion over the restricted angle of the movie lens—at the turning of a single crank. One does not need to be long upon a British battleship to find out that the inventive genius of the Anglo-Saxon race is not all confined to the American branch.

Between officers on watch and those resting to relieve, the after-dinner gathering around what had once been a fire was a small and rapidly dwindling one. As I got up to go to my cabin, the captain of marines quieted the pet cockatoo on his shoulder long enough to say, as we would probably be at "Action Stations" early in the morning, I might find it of interest to come up to his turret, where he had a "jolly smart crew." "We usually do 'B.J.1' at daybreak when we're out," he said, "just on the chance that we may flush some sort of a Hun in the early light. Quite like snipe-shooting, you know."

A "snotty" whom I met outside said something about the way the barometer had been chasing its tail on the drop ever since we got under weigh, and when I turned on the light in my cabin I noticed that the arrows on the navigating officer's instrument indicated a fall of thirty points since noon. The keen whistling of the rising wind shrilled with steady insistence, and the wide swinging swells from the open sea were lock-stepping along with a tread that was just beginning to lift the great warship in a swaggering Jack Tar roll.

On the floor of the cabin was a flannel bulldog with "manipulable" legs and a changeable expression. Its name was "Grip" (so "the pilot" had told me), and it had been his constant companion ever since it was presented to him on the eve of his first sailing as a midshipman. The only time they had ever been separated was on the occasion a colleague, who had borrowed it as a mascot in a game of poker, threw it overboard in chagrin when the attempt to woo fickle fortune proved a failure. Luckily, the ship was lying in a river, and the dog floated back on the next tide, and was fished out with no damage to anything but the compression bladder which worked its bark. The Navigating Officer left the companionable little beast in his cabin, so he explained, to give it the proper home touch for my first night at sea with the British Navy. Cocking "Grip" up in the genial glow of the electric grate in an attitude of "watchful waiting," I crawled into my bunk, pulled up the adjustable side-rail, and was rocked to sleep to the even throb of the turbines and the splish-splash of the spray against the screwed-down scuttle.

"We aren't having 'B.J.1' this morning," some one explained facetiously when I reported for "duty" at seven o'clock, "because we already have 'B.B.8.'" This last meant "Boreas Blowing Eight," he said, and I was just "nautical" enough to know that a wind of "8" in the Beaufort scale indicated something like fifty or sixty miles an hour.

"No U-boat will want to be getting within 'periscopic' distance of the surface of the sea that's running this morning," said a young engineer-lieutenant who had been in the submarine service, "and even if one was able to get a sight, its torpedo would have to have some kind of a 'kangaroo' attachment to jump the humps and hollows with. Fact is, it's rather more than our destroyers are entirely happy with, and we've just slowed down by several knots to keep 'em from dipping up the brine with their funnels. Hope nothing turns up that they have to get a jump on for. A destroyer's all right on the surface, but no good as a submarine; yet an under-sea diver is just what she is if you drive her more'n twelve into a sea like the one that's kicking up now. Barometer's down sixty points since last night, and still going."

Breakfast that morning had little in common with the similar festal occasion at Base where, fresh bathed and shaven, each immaculate member of the mess comes down and sits over his coffee and paper much (save for the fact that the journal is two days old) as at home. Several places besides those of the officers actually on watch were empty, and by no means a few of those who did appear had that introspective look which is so unmistakable a sign of all not being well within the citadel. Even the *Poldhu*—the daily wireless bulletin of the Navy—had a "shot-to-pieces" look where "static" or some other esoteric difficulty was responsible for gaps in several items of the laconic summary. The last word in super-dreadnoughts does not have table-racks and screwed-down chairs. She isn't supposed to lose her dignity to the extent of needing anything in the way of such vulgar makeshifts. The fact remains that if the mighty *Zeus* had chanced to have these things, she would have saved herself some china and several officers from "nine-pinning" down one side of a table and piling up in a heap at the end.

With the staid wardroom doing things like this, it was only to be expected that the mess decks would be displaying a certain amount of shiftiness. I was, however, hardly prepared for the gay seascape which unrolled before me when I had worried my way through the intricate barricade of a watertight bulkhead door in trying to skirmish forward to the ladders leading to the upper decks. For several reasons—ventilation and guns have something to do with it—it is not practicable to close up certain parts of a battleship against heavy seas to anything like the same extent as with the passenger quarters in a modern liner. It is only in very rough weather that this may give rise to much trouble, but—well, we were having rough weather that morning, and that little bit of the Roaring Forties I had stumbled into was a consequence of it.

Oilskinned, "sou'westered," sea-booted men, sitting and lying on benches and tables, was the first strange thing that came to my attention; and then, with a swish and a gurgle, the foot-deep wave of dirty water which had driven them there caught me about the knees, and sat me down upon a pile of hammocks, or, rather, across the inert bodies of two men (boys I found them to be presently) who had been cast away there in advance of me. Clambering over their unprotesting anatomies, I gained dry land at a higher level, and at a tactically defensible point, where a half-Nelson round a stanchion steadfastly refused to give way under the double back-action shuffle with which the next roll tried to break it. With two good toe-holds making me safe from practically anything but a roll to her beams' ends, I was free to survey the shambles at my leisure. Then I saw how the havoc was being wrought.

With a shuddering crash, the thousand-ton bludgeon of a wave struck along the port side, immediately followed by the muffled but unmistakable sound of water rushing in upon the deck above. To the accompaniment of a wild slap-banging, this sound came nearer, and then, as she heeled far to starboard under the impulse of the blow that had been dealt her, a solid spout of green water came tumbling down a hatchway—the fount from which the mobile tidal wave swaggering about the deck took replenishment. Two men, worrying a side of frozen Argentine bullock along to the galley from the cold-storage hold, timing (or, rather, mis-timing) their descent to coincide with that of the young Niagara, reached the mess-deck in the form of a beef sandwich. Depositing that delectable morsel in an inert mass at the foot of the ladder, the briny cascade, with a joyous whoof, rushed down to reinforce the tidal wave and do the rounds of the mess.

I was now able to observe that the sailors, marooned on the benches, tables, and other islands of refuge, were roughly dividable into three classes—the prostrate ones, who heaved drunkenly to the roll and took no notice of the primal chaos about them; the semi-prostrate ones, who were still able to exhibit mild resentment when the tidal wave engulfed or threatened to engulf them; and the others—some lounging easily, but the most perched or roosted on some dry but precarious pinnacle—who quaffed great mugs of hot tea and bit hungrily into hunks of bread and smoked fish. These latter—hard-bit tars they were, with faces pickled ruddy by the blown brine of many windy watches—took great joy of the plight of their mates, guffawing mightily at the dumb misery in the hollow eyes of the "semi-prostrates" and the dead-to-the-world roll of "prostrates" with the reelings of the ship.

If there is one thing in the world that delights the secret heart of the average landsman more than the sad spectacle of a parson in the divorce court, it is the sight of a sea-sick sailor. Since, however, the average landsman reads his paper far oftener than he sails the stormy seas, the former delectation is probably granted him rather more frequently than the latter. At any rate, the one landsman in No. X Mess of H.M.S. *Zeus* that morning saw enough sea-sick sailors to keep the balance on the parsons' side for the duration of the war, and perhaps even longer.

I made the acquaintance of one of the "prostrates" marooned on the beach of my hammock island through rescuing him from the assaults of a tidal-wave-driven rum tub. He was nursing a crushed package of gumdrop-like lozenges, one of which he offered me, murmuring faintly that they had been sent him by his sister, who had found them useful while boating at Clacton-on-Sea last summer. Endeavouring to start a conversation, I asked him—knowing the *Zeus* had been present at that mighty struggle—if they had had weather like this at the Battle of Jutland. A sad twinkle flickered for a moment in the corner of the eye he rolled up to me, and, with a queer pucker of the mouth which indicated that he must have had a sense of humour in happier times, he replied that he had only joined the ship the week before: "'Tis my first time at sea, sir, and I've come out to—to—this."

I gave him the best advice I could by telling him to pull himself together and get out on deck to the fresh air; but neither spirit nor flesh was equal to the initiatory effort. Looking back while I waited near the foot of a ladder for a Niagara to exhaust itself, the last I saw of him he was pushing mechanically aside with an unresentful gesture a lump of salt pork which one of the table-roosting sailors dangled before his nose on a piece of string.

Three flights up I clambered my erratic way before, on the boat deck in the lee of a launch, I found a vantage sufficiently high and sheltered to stand in comfort. The sight was rich reward for the effort. Save for an ominous bank of nimbus to westward, the wind had swept the coldly blue vault of the heavens clear of cloud, and the low-hanging winter sun to south'ard was shooting slanting rays of crystalline brightness across a sea that was one wild welter of cotton wool. I have seen—especially in the open spaces of the mid-Pacific, where the waves have half a world's width to get going in—heavier seas and higher seas than were running that morning, but rarely—not even in a West Indian hurricane—more vicious ones—seas more palpably bent on going over, or through a ship that got in their way, rather than under, as proper waves should do. And in this obliquity they were a good deal more than passively abetted by a no less viciously inclined wind, which I saw repeatedly lift off the top of what it appeared to think was a lagging wave, and drive it on ahead to lace the heaving water with a film of foam or dust the deck of a battleship with snowy brine.

But it was the ships themselves that furnished the real show. Of all craft that ply the wet seaways, the battleship is the least buoyant, the most "unliftable," the most set on bashing its arrogant way through a wave rather than riding over it, and—with the increasing armour and armaments, and the crowding aboard of various weighty contrivances hitherto unthought of—this characteristic wilfulness has tended to increase rather than decrease since the war. As a consequence, a modern battleship bucking its way into a fully developed mid-winter gale is one of the nearest approaches to the meeting of two irresistible bodies ever to be seen.

The conditions for the contest were ideal that morning. Never were seas more determined to ride over battleships, never were battleships more determined to drive straight through seas. Both of them had something of their way in the end, and neither entirely balked the other; but, drawn as it was, that battle royal of Titans was a sight for the gods.

The battleships were in line abreast as I came up on deck, and holding a course which brought the wind and seas abeam. We were all rolling heavily, but with the rolls not sufficiently "synchronised" with the waves—which were charging down without much order or rhythm—to keep from dipping them up by the ton. If the port rail was low—as happened when the ship was sliding down off the back of the last wave—the next wave rolled inboard, and (save where the mast, funnels, and higher works amidships blocked the way) drove right on across and off the other side. If the port side had rolled high as an impetuous sea struck, the latter expended its full force against the ship, communicating a jar from foretop to stokeholds as shivering as the shock of a collision with another vessel.

Our own quarter-deck was constantly swept with solid green water, and even the higher fo'c'sle deck caught enough of the splash-up to make traversing it a precarious operation. But it was only by watching one of the other ships that it was possible to see how the thing really happened. If it was the wallowing monster abeam to port, the striking of a sea was signalised by sudden spurts of spray shooting into the air all the way along her windward side, the clouds of flying water often going over the funnels and bridge, and not far short of the foretop. She would give a sort of shuddering stumble as the weight of the impact made itself felt, and then—running from bow to stern and broken only by the upper works, and occasionally, but not always, by the turrets—a ragged line of foam appeared, quickly resolving itself into three or four hundred feet of streaking cascades which came pouring down over the starboard side into the sea. Watching the vessel abeam to starboard, the phenomenon was repeated in reverse order. Save for the swaying foretop against the sky, either ship at the moment of being swept by a wave was suggestive of nothing so much as a great isolated black rock on a storm-bound coast.

But the most remarkable thing about it all was the astonishingly small effect this really heavy weather had upon the handling of the ships. Evidently they had been built to withstand weather as well as to fight, for they manœuvred and changed formation with almost the same meticulous exactitude as in protected waters. A gunnery officer assured me that—except for momentary interference in training some of the lighter guns—the fighting efficiency of the ship would hardly be effected by all their plungings and the clouds of flying spray. Their speed was, naturally, somewhat diminished in bucking into a head sea, yet no lack of seaworthiness would prevent (should the need arise) their being driven into that same head sea at the full power of their mighty engines. The reason we were proceeding at somewhat reduced speed was to ease things off a bit for the destroyers.

Ah! And what of the destroyers? There they all were, the faithful sheep-dogs, when I came up, and at first blush I got the impression that they were making rather better weather of it than the battleships. That this was only an optical illusion (caused by the fact that they were farther away and more or less obscured by the waves) I discovered as soon as I climbed to the vantage of the after super-structure, and put my glass upon the nearest of the bobbing silhouettes of mast and funnel. Then I saw at once, though not, indeed, any such spray clouds or cascades of solid water as marked the course of the battleships, that she was plainly a labouring ship. A destroyer is not made to pulverise a wave in the bull-at-a-gate fashion of a battleship, and any exigency that compels her to adopt that method of progression is likely to be attended by serious consequences. If one of the modern type she will ride out almost any storm that blows if left to her own devices; but force her into it at anything above half-speed, and it is asking for trouble. Even before the destroyer I was watching began disappearing—hull, funnels, and all but the mastheads—between crest and crest of the onrushing waves, it was plain that both she and her sisters were having all they wanted; and I was not surprised when word was flashed to us that one of our brave little watch-dogs was suffering from a wave-smashed steering geer, and had asked permission to make for port if necessary. The permission was, I believe, granted, but—carrying on with some sort of a makeshift or other—her plucky skipper managed to stick it out and see the game through to the end.

There were a number of other ships in difficulties in that neck of the North Sea at this moment, and every now and then—by the wireless—word would come to us from one of them. Mostly they were beyond the horizon, but two were in sight. One (two smoke-blackened "jiggers" and a bobbing funnel-top beneath a bituminous blur to the east) was apparently a thousand-ton freighter. An officer told me that she had been signalling persistently since daybreak for assistance; but when I asked him if we were not going to help her, he greeted the question with an indulgent smile.

"Assistance will go to her in due course," he said, "but it will not be from us. That kind of a thing might have been done in the first month or two of the war, but the Huns soon made it impossible. Now, any battleship that would detach a destroyer at the call of any ship of doubtful identity would be considered as deliberately asking for what she might jolly well get—a torpedo."

Another ship which was plainly having a bad time was some kind of a cruiser whose long row of funnels was punching holes in a segment of skyline. There was a suggestion of messiness forward, but nothing we attached any importance to until word was wirelessed that she had just had her bridge carried away by a heavy sea, and that the navigating officer had been severely injured. The latter was known personally to several of the wardroom officers, and at lunch speculation as to what hurt he might have received led to an extremely interesting discussion of the "ways of a wave with a man"; also of the comparative seaworthiness of light cruisers and destroyers. The things that waves have done to all three of them since the war began (to say nothing of the things all three have done in spite of waves) is a story of its own.

The barometer continued to fall all day, with the wind rising a mile of velocity for every point of drop. The seas, though higher and heavier, were also more regular and less inclined to catch the ship with her weather-rail down. The low cloud-bank of mid-forenoon had by early dusk grown to a heavens-obscuring mask of ominous import, and, by dark, snow was beginning to fall. The ship was reeling through the blackness of the pit when I clambered to the deck after dinner, so that the driving spray and ice-needles struck the face before one saw them by even the thousandth of a second. The darkness was such as one almost never encounters ashore, and it was some time before I accustomed myself to close my eyes against the unseen missiles (when turning to windward) without deliberately telling myself to do so in advance.

Into the Stygian pall the vivid golden triangles from the signal searchlights on the bridge flashed like the stab of a flaming sword. One instant the darkness was almost palpable enough to lean against; the next, the silhouette of funnels and foretop pricked into life, but only to be quenched again before the eye had time to fix a single detail. So brief was any one flash that the action in each transient vision was suspended as in an instantaneous photograph, yet the effect of the quick succession of flashes was of continuous motion, like the kinema. From where I stood, the heart of the fluttering golden halos, where a destroyer winked back its answer, were repeatedly obliterated by the inky loom of a wave, but the reflection was always thrown high enough into the mist to carry the message.

Returning to the wardroom by the way of the mess-decks, I saw the youth who had offered me the anti-seasick lozenges in the morning. Now quite recovered, he was himself playing the pork-on-a-string game with one of the only two "prostrates" still in sight. The following morning—though the weather, if anything, was worse than ever—all evidences of "indisposition" had disappeared.

For some days more we prowled the wet seaways, and then, well along into a night that was foggier, colder, and windier than the one into which we had steamed out, we crept along a heightening headland, nosed in the wake of the flagship through a line of booms, and opened a bay that was dappled with the lights of many ships. A few minutes later, and the raucous grind of a chain running out through a hawse-pipe signalled that we were back at the old stand.

And since, like all the rest of our sisters of the Grand Fleet, we were expected to be ready to put to sea on x hours' notice, there was nothing for it but that the several hundred tons of coal which the mighty *Zeus* had been snorting out in the form of smoke to contaminate the ozone of a very sizeable area of the North Sea should be replenished without delay. A collier edged gingerly out of a whirling snow-squall and moored fast alongside as I groped forward to retake possession of my cabin under the bridge, and I went to sleep that night to the grind of the winches and the steady tramp-tramp of the barrow-pushers on the decks below.

A NORTH SEA SWEEP

There are four sights in this war that have etched themselves more deeply upon the plates of my memory than any of a hundred others which are themselves unforgettable—my first heavy artillery bombardment in France, with a wallowing wave of men sweeping forward behind the smoke and dust clouds of an advancing barrage, the meteor trail across the northern sky of the first Zeppelin brought down over England, the fantastically foreshortened peaks of southern Macedonia—with Serb and Bulgar locked in death grips in the cockpit of a snow-choked valley—from an aeroplane, and the Grand Fleet taking form out of a North Sea mist on a winter's morning. And it is the last of these—though the only mind picture it has left is of endless lines of grey ships ploughing silently through grey waters to the blending line of sea and misty sky, while the others were pulsing with motion, vibrant with sound and vivid with the incomparable appeal of the drama in which the actors are fighting and falling, living and dying men—that stirs, and will stir, me longest and strongest of all.

Just why this is I cannot say, but some hint of it may be found in the fact—so well known to all lovers of the ocean—that with the sea it is more what one *feels* than what one *sees* that moves; and with the Grand Fleet, which is instinct with the soul of the sea which it commands, it is perhaps the feeling that a single sweep of the eye comprehends the one mightiest force in mankind's mightiest struggle, which invests those silent lines of steaming warships with a power to stir the imagination (in my own case at least) as nothing else on earth can stir it, nor—save only the sight of those same ships going into action to fulfil the purpose for which they were created—ever will.

My first sight of the Grand Fleet at sea I owe to the ready thoughtfulness which those who know him best so often refer to in speaking of Admiral Sir David Beatty. For three days I had been "standing by" on the —— waiting to go out into the North Sea on a jaunt which had been vaguely described to me as likely to develop "interesting possibilities," and that famous cruiser was under steaming orders at the moment an invitation came from the Flagship of one of the Battleship Squadrons to come over to a concert being given that afternoon aboard the "Theatre-Ship" *Gourko*. There was just time to take the show in before our departure the Captain of the —— reckoned, and volunteered to sail the Staff Surgeon and me over in his galley.

There was a notable attendance at the concert, and in the little company which were invited to Admiral Madden's cabin for tea, after the playing of

"God Save the King" and "The Star Spangled Banner" had signalised the end of an enjoyable programme, were at least a dozen men whose names would be entitled to head the list of the makers of modern naval history. While I was draining a single cup of tea I heard the Admiral who had won the Battle of the Falkland Islands explain the idiosyncrasies of North Sea meteorology; another, who had directed naval operations at the Dardanelles, expatiate on the difficulties of raising pigs on his Squadron's refuse since the "Food Economy" campaign got well under weigh in the Grand Fleet; a third, who had held high command at Jutland, outline a plan for elevating the popular taste for good music; and a fourth, who had done notable work at Dogger Bank, lay down the law on the points of Irish terriers. The only one whom I heard speak of "Things Naval" was the Commander-in-Chief, who was enticed into "shop" after inquiring how my plans were progressing in connexion with some voyages in light craft which I had asked permission to make.

On my telling him I expected to put to sea with the light cruisers in a couple of hours, he stood for a moment in thought, and then said quietly, "If you can throw your kit together and go aboard one of the battleships before the —— sails, I think that I can promise that you will see—in the course of the next thirty-six hours—a sight such as you have never seen before, one that you will never forget."

I hesitated for a moment, for a voyage in the historic ——, with the ever-present possibility of stumbling into an action with her, was something I had been planning for and counting upon for weeks.

"You can come out with us again in another week or so," said the Captain of the ——; "you may not be in a position to connect with what the Commander-in-Chief has to offer for a good deal longer than that."

"But my own ship is in quarantine," I said, suddenly recollecting that there had been a sporadic outbreak of mumps or something of the kind reported from the *Erin* in the course of the last day or two.

"Between thirty and forty capital ships, to say nothing of light cruisers and destroyers, we ought to be able to find room to stow you away for a couple of days," cut in Admiral Beatty with just the flicker of one of his rare smiles. "Let Captain —— arrange it for you. Perhaps Admiral Sturdee"—and a moment later the victor of the Battle of the Falklands was extending me a warm invitation to come to his Flagship as his guest for the events of the next few days. By dint of the liveliest kind of hustling, I was just able to return to the ——, get my togs picked up and clamber aboard the barge Admiral Sturdee had kindly despatched before the grinding of chains on hawse-pipes told that the light cruisers were shortening in preparatory to weighing anchor and departing on their own little North Sea sideshow.

An hour later I had climbed the gangway of my new ship, greeted several friends of a former visit in the wardroom, made a hurried shift of uniform in the comfortable cabin which had been prepared for me, and was seated at dinner with Admiral Sturdee and his Staff. Of the personal side of my voyage with this most highly distinguished and most deservedly loved of British admirals—an experience the more treasured in that it chanced to coincide with the last occasion on which he was destined to go to sea on active service before taking over an important command ashore—it is not my purpose to write here.

At another time, with Admiral Sturdee's concurrence, I shall endeavour to set down a few of the things—mostly reminiscent of events in which he had played an historic part, with occasional observations on international developments, political and social,—of which he spoke at table, in quiet intervals on the bridge, or while taking a few minutes' refuge from the wind in the cold little box of his Spartan sea-cabin.

There was nothing to differentiate our preparations for departure on the following afternoon from those for one of the several kinds of routine work that a squadron of battleships performs in the course of its regular duties. The "buzz" had gone around, however, that we were going out for a "P.Z."—a general exercise of all the units of the Battleship and Battle Cruiser fleets, with their auxiliaries—and the smoke which began rolling up from scores of funnels as the early afternoon hours wore on seemed to give confirmation to the theory that something was afoot which would result in the putting to sea of the massed might of the modern capital ships of the Navy. The British Lion was certainly going out on a prowl, and there was always the chance that he might be getting his claws into something. The infectious spirit of the "great game" blew like a fresh breeze through the mess-decks, and there was a new sparkle in every eye that met mine as I worked forward and upward to the fore bridge, a smile on every ruddy face, a jaunty set to every pair of swinging shoulders.

From the lofty vantage of the bridge I could see slim, gliding shapes—dusky Maltese against the brown-black background of a jutting headland—which were already threading the mazes of the booms, and knew that they were some of the sportive shoals of smaller craft—probably light cruisers—which would weave a far-flung circle of offence around the bulkier bullies of the Battle Fleet itself.

Now the long, low ships of a line that had been anchored for a mile on our starboard bow began slowly swinging in the boiling welter of reversed propellers, and then, when their dark noses were all pointing down the proper course as though strung on a single tow-line, they started in easy, effortless glide around the end of the squat, round-topped island which masked the exit through which they must pass.

"The 'Cats' are under weigh," said an officer at my elbow, pointing to where the graceful shadow of the *Tiger* and the grim profile of the *Lion* flitted in blank silhouette across a background, a stretch of cliff-begirt beach where the drifted snows of a recent storm still lay banked in a solid wall of dazzling white. Other shadows with historic names flashed into vivid contrast for a few moments, and then dissolved into misty indistinctness as they passed on to where their protective colouring merged with the watery background; and behind these glided the silhouettes of other ships which I knew to be "super-cats," ships with names yet unknown to fame, but which were reputed to be able to outrun and outclaw their predecessors by as wide a margin as they outbulked them. One by one the gaunt profiles sharpened into sudden brightness and then died down like the lights of a train dashing across a trestle into a deep cut.

"It will be our turn presently," the Flag Lieutenant said, as he turned a sheaf of signals just passed up to him. "Each division gets under weigh to a time-table, and any substantial deviation from this by even one ship would upset the schedule for all of the Squadrons following."

A quick order, the breaking out of a string of signal flags, the jerky, serpentine inrush of the already shortened anchor-chain, and our ship had caught the impulse of her accelerating screws and began slowly gathering headway. Down past the head of line after line she steamed, the men of each ship as she came abreast standing at attention to salute the Flag of the Admiral. Eight ships in "Line Ahead," the Squadron glided easily up the flow toward the gate.

As we passed one great tower of steel after another a breezy midshipman began speaking of their "points" and "records" as he might have reviewed the exhibits at a Bench Show. There was the *Marlborough*, which the Germans had "sunk" with a torpedo at Jutland, and there—"that cubistic nightmare" (referring to her scientific camouflage)—the new "———," which was supposed to "absorb" torpedoes as a Stilton cheese does port, and to improve day by day under the treatment. "The *matlotes* will tell you," he said, "that she goes off and mooches round the U-boat lanes just to tempt them to use up their mouldies on her so that there won't be so many left for merchant ships!"

And there was the ——, and he went on to tell me of one of her gunners who, writing home after the battle, had stated that there was a time when he had been unable to make his way aft from his turret on account of the heaps of dead bodies blocking the way.

"You know very well that we were not hit during the battle," the irate Captain, before whom the culprit had been forthwith, admonished. "What prompted you to tell such a mischievous lie?"

"I was upholding the glory of the Gran' Fleet, Sir," was the unabashed answer. "I couldn't bear to 'ave 'em thinkin' at 'ome that the blinkin' battle cruisers 'ad been 'avin' all the fun o' the go."

Another even line of foretops, seeming to float through the air above the skyline of an interposing island like a file of flying geese, told us, as we cleared the barrage, that another Squadron was getting under weigh; but these, with the "Cats" creeping off under their back-blown smoke trails, into a bank of purple mist, were all that were in sight when the swift winter twilight shut down and left us ploughing alone down the lane between our screening destroyers.

It was just at this time—in the short 'tween-daylight-and-dark interval—that a strange thing happened. The sea was smooth, silken smooth, with hardly more than an eight- or ten-knot breeze ruffling its surface, and the ship was—so far as pitch or roll were concerned—as steady as though chocked up in a dry dock. Suddenly, a couple of cables' lengths ahead, a thin white line of foam appeared, serpentining along at about right angles to our course. It appeared to be quite the same sort of little froth-path that one has come to know in the seas of all the world as the marker of the place where tide meets tide, a phenomenon indicating conflicting but rarely dangerous countercurrents.

I noted that a half-dozen glasses were trained on the wriggling streak, and was wondering what there could be about it to excite such anxious interest, when the Flotilla Leader on our port bow swung swiftly round through eight or ten points and came charging straight down towards us. No helm ever spun a ship like that, I told myself, even before the violently tossing foam geyser under the "amok's" stern revealed that both helm and screws were doing their utmost to throw her back toward her original course. I had barely time to observe with astonishment that the destroyer on our starboard bow was plunging off in a totally different direction than her "opposite number," when an invisible hand seemed to reach up from below and seize our ship in its vice-like grip. Round swung that 25,000 tons of steel without offering any more apparent resistance than a drifting skiff or a floating log.

There was no knowing until that instant which way the ship was going to swing, and the Chief Navigating Officer's sharp "Hard-a-port!" down the voice-pipe was the only order there was any use in giving, when it became clear that we were being turned six or eight points to port on a course calculated to present pretty much of her whole starboard side for the oncoming destroyer to flatten itself against. The grind of the labouring helm ran like a shudder from stern to bow, but the avoidance of a collision was up to the destroyer rather than the battleship.

Out of the tail of my eye (as I focussed my attention on more imminent developments) I saw that the other battleships and destroyers were cutting capers similar to our own. No two of the dozen or more craft appeared to be steering the same course, and one or two of the destroyers, like helplessly skidding motors on a muddy street, had actually turned through thirty-two points and were heading back on their proper courses.

It was not an especially close call with our Flotilla Leader after all, for her helm cut into water, "standing still" sufficiently to give it a grip, while she yet had room to clear our swinging bows by a score of yards. Wallowing enormously, she spun swiftly round and darted back to her station, while the more ponderous battleship was still reeling dazedly like a half-drunken man trying to orientate after picking himself up from a fall. Then, silently and mysteriously as they had come, the treacherous swirls and eddies rolled on, and ten minutes later—a row of blurred black towers dimly discernible against the falling curtain of the night,—the Squadron was again in "Line Ahead" and steaming quietly toward the open sea in its wonted order.

"In its way, this is quite the nastiest bit of water in all the world," said Admiral Sturdee, turning from the rail of the bridge with an expression of relief on his face. "There is a number of places where the tides run more swiftly than here, but none (in my own experience at least) where they run in so many directions at the same time. The waters for miles are a continual succession of giant whirlpools. These make navigation difficult and uncertain all over the Firth, but in the zone of the tide-rip (as you have just seen) they are infernal. Sometimes—even in stormy weather—we go out without having any trouble whatever at the 'rip'; again, as to-day, with little wind and less sea, it picks up a squadron of warships aggregating over two hundred thousand tons in displacement, and shakes them like a terrier worrying a string of sausages. When it's in this kind of a temper, threading the passages at the entrance of a South Pacific coral atoll (to most sailors the last thing in difficult navigation) is like sailing down a countryside canal in comparison. Have you ever seen anything like it?"

"Never at sea," I replied. "Indeed, the only time—anywhere—I ever saw waters take such wanton liberties with craft trying to navigate them was in the White Horse Rapids of the old Klondike route, and those boats were only twenty or thirty-footers of green whipsawed lumber. But aren't there certain kinds of weather when it is next to physically impossible for any kind of a ship to live here? When you get a well-developed gale blowing against the tide, for instance?"

"Ah, that's the combination that does it," said the Admiral with a grim smile, turning to go down to the Chart House with the Flag Captain. "You remember what happened to those two destroyers here in that blow of eight or ten days ago (only one survivor out of the crews of both), and you might ask X—— to tell you what befell the old '——' the night she started out into a storm."

The Flag Lieutenant came and leaned against the rail at my side. "It must have happened just about where we are now," he said, rubbing a cinder down into the inner corner of his eye and out on the bridge of his nose in approved fashion. "The tide-rip may ambush you almost anywhere inside of here, and—especially if the weather is thick—you are lucky if your ship doesn't end up somewhere along the forty or fifty miles of cliffy coast that hems in this accursed pocket of water. The old '——' did not go ashore, but her case is notable as being probably the worst bit of bashing a battleship ever had from seas alone.

"She was going out by herself—bound for the Mediterranean, if I remember rightly—and what happened is probably largely due to the fact that they drove her, with the tide, into the teeth of the storm (perhaps to get out where there was more sea-room as quickly as possible) instead of slowing down and taking it easy, as we would be inclined to do now, even with ships a good deal bigger and more powerful. Most of these things have to be learned by experience, and if the '——' hadn't learned the lesson and paid the price, probably one of the others of us would have had to.

"At any rate, she bucked right into a mountain of a wave that swept her with hundreds—perhaps thousands—of tons of solid green water. When it had passed, her bridges and superstructures—everything, indeed, but her mast and turrets—was crushed down and carried away. A number of men went over the side with the wreckage, and most of those above decks not carried away were killed. The Captain was picked up on the quarterdeck, alive but with his legs broken. Nothing but a battleship could have survived such a blow, though it is quite possible that a more buoyant craft would have ridden higher over the wave and so shipped less solid water. I have seen a good many warships that have dragged themselves back to port after a battle, but never a one that presented such a sight as the poor old '——' did when she limped home the morning after the night before. She is still in commission, I believe, but there can't be an unreplaced rivet in her that doesn't have a crook in its neck to remind it that something hit her that night in Pentland Firth."

The Flag Lieutenant turned his glass for a moment toward a succession of flashes, in which a destroyer was pouring out its troubles to us from the outer darkness, and then leaned back on the rail again. "It would be hard to say whether the Firth is really our worst enemy or our best friend," he resumed presently. "There is a good deal to be said on both sides. First and last, it has probably bashed us about a good deal more than the Hun has; but, at the same time, there is no use denying that it has prevented him from making us a good deal of trouble he might have made if there had been an ordinary respectable sheet of water running right up to the front door of our refuge.

"In the first year of the war we used to let off guns at periscopes and the wash of conning towers every few days in the Firth, and the very enterprising U-boat to which they were supposed to belong came to be known by the nickname of the *Pentland Pincher*. Before very long, however, we learned that the supposed periscopes were only the necks of swimming cormorants, and the 'conning tower washes' certain characteristic little humps of Pentlandesque waves. We also learned—in one way or another—that a U-boat would have about as much chance of running submerged through one of those googly tide-rips as it would have of ascending the Thames to London, while for it to go down and try to rest on the bottom would be about like a Zeppelin trying to come to roost among the splintered peaks of the Dolomites. Indeed, the best way for you to visualise the bottom of Pentland Firth is to think how the Bernese Oberland looks from the summit of the Matterhorn. It is the currents of the Atlantic and the North Sea rendezvousing over such a bottom which makes the Pentland Firth what is probably the most temperamental bit of water in the Seven Seas."

With scarcely a motion, save the quiet insistent urge of the spinning turbines—something sensed rather than felt, save in the after part of the ship—we ploughed on into a night that required small effort to fancy as filched from a Mediterranean April or a North Pacific June. The breeze—no more than a zephyr purring contentedly over our starboard quarter—was redolent with the "landsy" smell of the North Scottish hills, and the indolent ebony billow heaving in from the North Sea had just enough energy to rise with a friendly swish and blink blandly up at us through the "eye-holes" of the hawse-pipes.

"We're watching you," those transient foam flashes seemed to signal, "but we're not going to try to do anything to disturb you, leastways not to-night. Might just as well make a stand-easy of your watch."

It must have been the almost tropical mildness of the night which turned the Admiral's mind, after he had rejoined us on the bridge, back to his days in the South Seas. Leaning lightly on the rail, and with only an occasional step aside for a squint at the soft round glow of the binnacle, or a swift glance to where barely discernible flashes of white revealed the bow-wave and wake of a screening destroyer, he spoke of the stirring events of ninety-nine when, commanding H.M.S. *Porpoise*, and weeks away from the nearest cable, he had co-operated with the American naval forces there in an endeavour to save the Samoas from the grip of a far extended tentacle of the German octopus, already stirring in its slime and reaching outwards to fasten its hold upon any of the desperately desired "sun-places" its suckers might encounter.

On a later occasion Admiral Sturdee narrated at length the events of the astonishing drama that was played out by the reef and palm of fair Apia, and dwelt on the significance which attached to them in the light of later developments; but for the moment—under the influence of this "maverick" of a tropic night that had strayed into a North Sea January—it was of the softer side of the idyllic South Pacific existence that he spoke. The Chief Navigating Officer, who had once been in a cruiser on the Australian station, came and joined us when his watch was over, and for an hour—or was it two or three?—we talked of *siva-sivas* and *hulas*, of swims with the village maidens in the pool under the sliding waterfall of Papa-sea; of moonlight dances under the coco-palms of Tutuila, of *kava* drinking and *luaus* of hot-stone-roasted sucking pig; of missionaries, traders, and "black-birders"; of Stevenson, Louis Becke, and "Bully" Hayes; of the thousand and one customs and characters, dangers and delights, that go to complete the idyll in those sensuous latitudes fanned by the perfumed breath of the South-East "Trade."

The Admiral was just telling of his youthful embarrassment the first time the *taupo* or village maiden of Apia insisted on encircling his neck with the same fragrant garland of *Tiare Tahiti* which was looped around her own, when a signal was brought him by the Flag Lieutenant. He read it by the reflected light from the binnacle, grinned amusedly, and handed it to the Flag Captain. The ripple of a quick smile ran over the grave countenance of the latter, and the play of light and shadow on two or three other faces which pushed into the pale glow of the binnacle seemed to indicate that the signal was something out of the regular routine orders. Presently the Admiral beckoned me inside the glassed-in bridge cabin and handed me the sheet of white paper. This, as nearly as may be set down, was what I read.

"S.N.O. at —— reports unusual sound in hydrophones. Supposed to be hostile submarine —— miles S.E. of —— Island."

"—— miles sou'-east of —— Island," mused the Admiral. "H'm. Just about the position of the Squadron at the present moment. H'm.... Think I may as well go down and get a few hours' sleep. Have to turn out early in the morning. Be sure and be up here at daybreak," he added, turning to me. "Perhaps you'll find the sea will not be quite as empty then as it seems to be to-night."

Giving my arm a friendly squeeze in passing, he disappeared down the ladder, followed by his Flag Lieutenant.

"The Admiral doesn't appear to be much disturbed about that U-boat we are supposed to be steaming over," I remarked to the Commander, who had come up a few minutes previously.

"What U-boat?" he asked. "Oh, the one in the signal. Well, hardly. He knows by long experience that the average U-boat skipper won't take any risks he can avoid with a warship behind a destroyer screen, especially where there is a chance of throwing his mouldies into some merchantmen and drowning a lot of women and children. There is only one thing the Hun is more careful about than his torpedoes, and that is his own thick hide."

The waning moon had risen just before midnight, and my last look round before turning in revealed, to port, one line of destroyers—swift, blue-grey arrows—shooting smoothly along in the light of it, and, to starboard, another line of dark shadows silhouetted against the silvered waters to the south-east, with the leader cutting a fluent furrow across the moon-track itself.

The "To-ra-loo" of the imperious call to "Action Stations" awoke me before dawn on the following morning, and it was through a tangle of men, hammocks, and unreeling fire-hose, and in the bedlam of clanging water-tight doors and the banging of hurrying feet upon steel ladders, that I wriggled forward and upward toward the fore bridge. The sharp blast which cut my face as I emerged upon the boat deck gave warning that the weather had indulged in one of its sudden overnight changes, and that the day would be one of characteristic North Sea rawness. Ducking through a fluttering string of mounting bunting on the signal bridge, I gained the next ladder and came out upon the fore bridge, with an open view before me at last.

Early as it was, Admiral Sturdee was there before me, and wearing no more protection against the penetrating cold than was afforded by an ordinary service cap and uniform, a short overcoat, and a light pair of overshoes. In contrast, I felt almost ashamed of the ponderous duffle coat—a half-inch thick of solid wool, and equipped with a heavy hood—with which I had fortified myself against the weather.

"You're just in time," he greeted me cheerily with. "Come and look who's here."

It was an ashen grey morning, with a low mist just beginning to thin into luminous strata in the light of the rising sun. Overhead it was clear, with indications good for a brightening all around before long. At first I was conscious of only the ships of our own Squadron, with those of the Second Division steaming hard to close up the "night interval" between them and those of the First. Then, abeam to port, I espied a similar line, and beyond that another and still another. And farther still, slipping ghostly along in the depths of the retreating mist, was even another line.

"Shades of Father Neptune!" I gasped. "Do they go on into the Skager Rak? Where did they all come from?"

The Admiral smiled, led me over to the starboard side, and pointed to where, dimly discernible against the smoke pall with which they had smudged the immaculate south-eastern heavens, but still unmistakable, was a file of great ships driving hard to push up to their appointed station.

"Some of them have come a long way,"[B] he said, with a twinkle in his steady grey eye, "but we're all the gladder to have them here. As for the others," he went on, going back to the port side, "we're almost at the extreme right of our present formation, and, until the sun licks up a bit more of this mist, you will not be able to see more than halfway across the Battle Fleet, to say nothing of the battle cruisers and all the other ships that are out to-day. It's far from being a favourable morning on which to have your first view of the Grand Fleet at sea; just about the same shifting sort of visibility, indeed, that we had at Jutland."

"It may be so," I assented; "yet to me there is a suggestion of going-on-to-the-ends-of-the-earth in the way those farthest lines melt into the mist that would be quite absent if it was clear enough really to see the last of them. As it is, it takes no effort at all of the imagination to fancy those lines going on, and on, and on, into the farthest bight of the farthest sea in which their power is felt. I wouldn't have a clear horizon for the world to-day. The Grand Fleet will never be so big to me as it is this morning. I know just how big it is (for I've learned the names of all its units, ship by ship), and I know just about how much sea it takes up (for I've looked down on the whole of it from a 'kite' at Scapa); but to-day—to me—it reaches to the ends of the Seven Seas, and I don't want any shifting of the scenery to destroy my illusion."

The Fates were kind, for that mask of luminous mist (though it interfered considerably with the effectiveness of the "P.Z." as an exercise) did not clear away sufficiently during all the time we were out to make it possible to see, from even the loftiest vantage, the whole of the Fleet at one time. So that first illusion still holds, and so strongly that I cannot visualise it—even to-day, many weeks after—without a catch in my breath and a "choky" feeling in the throat. I have seen "all the way across" the Grand Fleet several times in the interim, and once I have been with it when it tore across the North Sea on what appeared the hottest kind of a scent; and yet—that first impression has kept a place all its own.

Straight on eastward pressed the swiftly steaming Fleet, straight on into the alternately advancing and receding mist wall, until the snowbirds from the "other side"—wind-blown victims of the capricious shift of weather—were fluttering about our bows, and the blurred outline of what appeared to be a rocky coast rose distantly in the smother ahead. Then, at a signal from the Flagship, we turned ten or a dozen points and stood away to the south on a course that might lead anywhere from the Skager Rak to Heligoland Bight. *That* manœuvre would have been a sight for a clear to-day, and to be followed from a balloon, if one were to have his choice of vantages. A hundred ships—more or less—were steering steadily on one course. Suddenly a string of multi-coloured bunting breaks out beside the half-blurred blue-black tower of a unit steaming somewhere toward the middle of the formation, and instantly the whole great body begins to turn. Vastly more than a million tons of steel are wheeling in unison at the flutter of that single signal, and yet in any one ship no more than a few quiet words down a voice-pipe—orders less loud and no more peremptory than that with which one would bring his spaniel to heel—have been spoken.

"Steady by compass!" you hear (if you chance to be standing close to the quiet-voiced Chief Navigating Officer bending above the binnacle); and presently, "Port fifteen!" At practically the same moment those same orders have been given on the leading battleship of every line, and round they go together, throwing swirling wakes with short sharp waves running off their outer curves and transiently smooth patches in the embrace of the inner ones. When the turn is complete and the leading ships ploughing the desired course, the laconic "Midships" completes the brief series of orders.

To a novice the countless destroyers shuttling in every direction between, ahead, and astern of the turning lines of battleships and wallowing wildly in the confused welter of conflicting wakes appear to be wheeling as aimlessly as range cattle "milling" in a blizzard. In reality their moves are calculated to a nicety, and they turn and "click" to place with almost the precision of the plungers of the combination of a safe.

The "flexibility" of the Grand Fleet, in spite of its increasing size—it has seldom if ever gone to sea but what it was stronger by many thousands of tons than when it last emerged—is a source of never-ending wonder to one to whom it has not become a commonplace by endless repetition, and the swiftness and ease with which it changes form at the will of the Commander-in-Chief never fails to remind me of one of those fascinating wire toys which an ingenious child can push or pull into a great variety of geometrical shapes. A few points' alteration of course changes a squadron—or a half dozen of them steaming abreast—into any desired "Line of Bearing," which might be what would happen in case it was deemed advisable to start zigzagging to avoid a submarine. A squadron may go from "Line Ahead" to "Line Abreast" in anywhere from a few seconds to a few minutes, according to the course the latter is going to hold, and so on through other formations, simple and complex. How this works in practice I had a good opportunity to see before we returned to Base.

The general practice on a "P.Z." for the Grand Fleet is to make a comprehensive sweep around the North Sea for two or three or four days, and then—if none of the enemy has been caught up in the net—to chivy together as large a force as possible of battle cruisers, light cruisers, and anything else available and have a sham fight with them. Failing in the former on this occasion, recourse had been had to the latter, and our Squadron was just getting ready to "open" on some dusky, mist-masked shapes suspected of being the "enemy," when the incident occurred to which I have referred.

"To 'equalise' the opposing forces," Admiral Sturdee was explaining to me, "it is laid down that each ship in the Fleet we are meeting shall represent a Squadron of the enemy. For instance, that light cruiser to the right—the one making all that smoke—represents an 'enemy' Battleship Squadron, which, incidentally, is steaming hard in the hope of getting in a position to waft us a breeze on a 'windy corner' when we begin to turn. Incidentally"—and the lines of his firm mouth relaxed in a quick smile—"I think we shall have turned before he gets to the place he's driving for. Now that ship there (I think she's a battle cruiser) represents——"

Just then his Flag Lieutenant, stepping rather more quickly than usual, handed him a signal. "Now fancy that," he said, after running his eye over the laconic message; "there's an enemy submarine ahead of us."

"And what might she represent, sir?" I asked, my mind still engrossed with the intricate strategy of the "battle" into which we were rushing at twenty knots an hour.

The Admiral had turned to read a second signal—this one from the Flagship—after which he was busy giving some orders on his own account.

My very natural query would have remained unanswered had it not been overheard by the Commander, who had just come up from below.

"Officially," he said with a laugh, "she probably represents the Kaiser, or Von Tirpitz, or whoever stands sponsor for the Huns' 'ruthless' submarine war. That signal refers to a U-boat, not to any of the craft playing in our little game." He paused for a moment as a detonation of terrific force rumbled distantly, and a shock like that of a blow from a mighty wave shook the ship from bow to stern, and then resumed with a grim smile: "But if that charge came anywhere near her, by this time she probably represents—well, a tired lily folding up and going to sleep for the night would probably be about as near it as anything in Nature."

Eight or ten times, with short intervals between, those thunderous undersea detonations—each followed by its own shuddering jar—came over and through the water to us. Whitish perpendicular bars, dimly guessed in the mist, revealed what might have been high-tossed foam-geysers four or five miles away, but it was almost inconceivable that explosions at that distance could reach us with such staggering force. Indeed, I have since talked with officers from a number of different squadrons—seasoned veterans of many big gun battles, all of them—who, experiencing the shocks from 'tween decks, felt certain that their own ships had been mined or torpedoed.

While the muffled booms of the depth-charges were still sounding we saw one of the "enemy" ships—apparently a battleship of the "Queen Elizabeth" class—which had been manœuvring for a position from which she could deliver an effective "broadside" at us, suddenly alter course eight points to port and head directly away at right angles to our extended line. As the raking this would have exposed her to was about the last thing in the world she would have risked had she been still playing the "make believe" battle, it hardly needed the far-borne and faint but still unmistakable shriek of a syren to tell us there was another game afoot. Presently she altered back to her original course, and all we ever heard of what happened was a signal, received shortly afterwards, saying that the *Valiant* had attempted to ram the periscope of a hostile submarine.

From first to last this little by-play had taken but a very few minutes, and, absorbed in the drama being played out on the fringes of the mist curtain, I quite neglected to take account of what was going on in our immediate vicinity. When I looked again the disposition of the units of the Grand Fleet—both battleships and screening destroyers—had completely altered. The battle formation had melted as by magic into one which offered the maximum of protection against submarine attack. Shortly we went down to lunch, where the only allusion I recall being made to the episode was something Admiral Sturdee said about how discouraging it must have been to the U-boat skipper to bob up right in the middle of the Grand Fleet, and then not have an opportunity to fire a single torpedo. In the afternoon we crept upon the "skeleton" fleet of the "enemy" in the mist and gave it the trouncing the U-boats were responsible for our failing to complete in the morning. The next day the Grand Fleet was lying quietly at its anchorage.

FOOTNOTES:

[B] The reference is to the ships of the ——th or American Battle Squadron, which went to sea with the Grand Fleet for the first time on this occasion.

A VISIT TO THE BRITISH FLEET

While lunching with Admiral Sir Doveton Sturdee in the course of a recent visit to the Grand Fleet, which must always remain one of the most memorable experiences of my life, I ventured the opinion that the work of the British Navy in sweeping every enemy vessel—warship and merchant steamer—from the surface of the Seven Seas, was the one most outstanding achievement of the war.

"Perhaps you are right," said the victor of the Battle of the Falklands thoughtfully, "but you must not lose sight of the fact that to win this victory over the German the British sailor has had to win an even more remarkable victory over himself. At the outbreak of the war I had every confidence that, in one way or another, we would be able to establish a control of the sea quite as complete as that which we actually have established; but, if any one could have assured me that the foundations of that control would have to rest upon the Grand Fleet being based in this isolated harbour, with the men practically cut off from intercourse with the world for months at a time, I must confess that I might have been—well, somewhat less sure, to say the least. Certainly I would never have dared more than to hope that the moral of the men of the Fleet, far from being lowered by the most trying experience of the kind sailors have ever been called upon to endure, would actually be heightened. On the score of enthusiasm and 'lust for battle,' there could not, of course, have been any improvement, but this has given way to a cheerful, high-spirited willingness which, if possible, makes the Fleet a more efficient fighting unit with every day that passes. If you will observe well the spirit of the men of the Grand Fleet at a time when the German Fleet—based though it is in the Kiel Canal, where regular shore-leave is easy to arrange—is filled with unrest and threatened with mutiny, I think you will agree with me the keeping of the British sailor in a healthy state of mind and body, without once letting him verge on 'staleness,' is worthy to rank as an achievement with that of keeping the enemy off the seas."

Evidence of the high spirits of the men of the Grand Fleet I had been having from the moment I sighted the first car-load of returning-from-leave sailors on my journey up from London, but the occasion on which I was the most impressed was the morning on which I was allowed the honour of helping to coal ship by wheeling 2-cwt. sacks on a barrow for a couple of hours, an experience the memory of which promises long to outlast even the not unlingering stiffness of my dorsal muscles. The ship had not been ordered, and was not expecting to be ordered to sea, and there was no reason to rush the coaling save to be free to take up some other of the regular grind of routine drudgery next in order.

I have watched warships coaling in many ports of the world, but never have I seen men working under the stimulus of extra shore-leave at Gibraltar, Nagasaki, or Valparaiso get the stuff into bunkers faster than did those lusty men of the good old "X——" that misty morning in Scapa Flow. Almost every man who was not smoking was singing, and even out of the dust-choked inferno of the collier's holds, the beat of a chesty chorus welled up in the pauses of the grinding winches.

Time and again (until I learned how to defeat the manœuvre) men behind me in the line pushed their barrows in ahead and made off with sacks that should have been mine to shift, and time and again (until I had found my second wind and my "coaling legs") the rollicking Jack Tar just behind me put his speeding barrow into one of my by no means slow-moving heels. The several hundred tons of coal which went down the chutes between 7 a.m. and 9 a.m. on that ordinary "routine" morning was shifted at a rate that would have been entirely creditable to a crew filling their bunkers for a long-deferred homeward voyage.

I did not have another opportunity to discuss with Admiral Sturdee the manner in which the miracle of "Fleet moral" had been wrought, but an officer of the battleship in which I stayed summed the thing up succinctly.

"I quite understand," I had said, "why the physical health of the Fleet should be the best ever known—why no battleship averages more than two or three sick at a time. The long months away from the germ-laden air of the land is sufficient to account for that. But how, after these three years and a half between the Devil, the Deep Sea, and the Scotch Mist, the men are still exuberant enough to want to push barrows of coal faster than a landsman, like myself (who is pushing for the sheer luxury of the thing), or how they are still full enough of *joie de vivre* to enjoy fits of singing between fits of coughing in the hold of a collier, is beyond my comprehension. How did you do it?"

The reply was prompt and to the point, and seems to me to disclose the secret in a nutshell. "By giving them," he said, "both more work and more play than they had in peace-time; in other words, by cutting down to a minimum the time in which to twirl their thumbs and think."

"Outside polishing brass and holystoning the deck," he went on, "there is a deal more work in a warship in war-time than in days of peace, so that we are never hard put to find a field for extra effort. We learn much quicker from practice than we did from theory, and there is an astonishing amount of work going on all the time to the end that the ship shall be kept as up to date as possible in all her equipment. The increase of a ship's offensive and defensive power, making her better to fight with and safer to fight in, is naturally a work in which the men are vitally interested, and they go into it with a will. We try as far as possible to avoid simply putting the men through the motions of work, like doing unnecessary painting or scrubbing, for instance. If the ship does not provide for the moment enough real work, we try to find it on the beach. For the next few days, for example, we are sending several hundred men ashore to make roads on one of the islands. They are very keen about the change, and I have heard them speaking about it all to-day. That kind of a thing works much better than simply improvising work on board. It gives variety, and the men feel that they are doing something useful instead of simply being kept busy.

"So much for work. On the score of play, we aim to give the men rather more athletic sports than they would have in harbour in peace-time, though all of it has to be carried on with many less 'frills'—flag-dressings, tea-parties, and the like—under the limiting conditions of always being ready to put to sea at notice of a few hours. In the ship, doubling round the deck for exercise is kept up regularly, as is also a certain number of Swedish drills. Every encouragement is given to the men to box, and the ship, squadron, and Fleet championships in the various classes are, of course, great events. There is scarcely a drifter or patrol-boat without one or more sets of boxing-gloves, for there is no form of sport quite so well calculated to exercise both mind and body in restricted quarters.

"Water-sports—swimming, rowing, and sailing—are kept up about as in peace-time, though here the long spell of inclement weather makes the winter rather a longer 'closed season' than farther south. Ashore there are several indifferent cricket and football grounds, though not, however, nearly enough for the normal demand of the great number—it runs well up into six figures—of able-bodied, sport-loving men in the Fleet. A good deal of hockey is played, and we have found it a better wet-weather game than football. In all of these sports inter-ship and inter-squadron rivalry is encouraged, principally because it stimulates the minds of so many outside the actual participants.

"Many of the officers have their golf clubs and tennis racquets, and though our links and courts would hardly satisfy the critical eyes of St. Andrews or 'Queens' professionals, they have been a big help to us. Cross-country runs and paper-chases, up and down the steep hills and over the soggy peat bogs, are taken part in by both men and officers, and for flesh-reducing, muscle-hardening, and chest-expanding are about the best thing we have. The tug-of-war is a traditional Navy sport, for it can, if necessary, be enjoyed on shipboard as well as ashore. The great pride which the men of a ship take in the success of its team makes this also a very useful sport for its 'psychologic' value.

"Amusements pure and simple—the kinema and theatricals—are a new thing with us (at least while on active service) and the scheme is still in process of development. For a number of reasons it is impracticable for professional troupes to visit the Grand Fleet in the same way as they have been going to France to entertain the Army. The greater distance is against it, as is also the fact that we have no place to put them up. Again, as there is no place where they could perform to more than a thousand men (at the outside) at one time, it would obviously take some months to make a round of the Fleet. The fact that the visitors might awake almost any morning to find themselves on the way to a sea-fight is also a deterrent. All of these things have made it necessary for us to shift for ourselves in the matter of entertainment.

"Each ship, of course, has always had its band and orchestra, and concerts and rather crude theatrical shows have been features of Navy life from time immemorial. The trouble with the shows, however, has always been the amount of improvising that they entailed, especially in the matter of a stage, footlights, seats, and the like. Before the war the men usually managed to find time to paint and rig 'flies' and 'drops,' devise lighting effects, and even to fix up some kind of 'auditorium.' Here, with the whole ship standing by for orders to put to sea, all of this was out of the question. Under these circumstances, the man who first conceived the idea of a special 'theatre ship' deserves a monument as a benefactor to the British Navy.

"The suggestion was to provide a steamer on which a permanent stage, complete with sets of scenery, exits and entrances, footlights, sidelights, and dressing-rooms, had been installed; also sufficient seats to accommodate as many of the crew of a battleship as could ever be off duty at one time. The thing would have been worth while a dozen times over, even if it had been necessary to detach a three or four thousand-ton steamer for no other purpose. Luckily, the plan chanced to dove-tail to a nicety with the functions of a steamer which, in carrying frozen beef to the Fleet, laid alongside each ship for from twenty-four to forty-eight hours. The stage, auditorium, and the rest were built without interfering in the least with the steamer's regular work, nor have the some hundreds of performances already given aboard been responsible for the least interruption in our supply of frozen beef. As for the shows, she is discharging to the 'X——' of our squadron to-day, and you can go over to-night and see one for yourself.

"The trouble with the 'theatre ship' idea is that it is too long between shows. Between the battleship and the endless auxiliaries, it may easily take from two to three months for the beef-cum-theatre steamer to make the full round of the Fleet, an interval which we had to find some way of bridging with other entertainment. It was a difficult problem in many ways, and it is only within the last month or two that we have found—through the kinema—a satisfactory solution. Every ship in the Fleet has now its projector, and, through an organisation formed in London for that purpose, a continuous supply of the latest and best films is sent up and circulated at a cost to us that is almost negligible. The films on arrival at the Depot Ship which houses the Post Office, are listed and filed, to be distributed to the various units in accordance with their demands.

"Each ship has a daily bulletin of the new films arriving, and at once sends in an application for its preference, with two or three alternatives should the first choice have gone to a prior claimant. The scheme has been successful beyond words. Each ship has a nightly performance, the projector being at the disposal of the men during the week, and of the officers on Saturday. All share in the cost of it, which only comes to a shilling or two per head a month. With a little larger supply of the more popular films, the development of this kinema scheme promises to give us everything we could possibly ask on the score of evening amusement. About the only thing left to do would be to buy a few picture-taking machines, let the officers and men write the scenarios, and start making films on our own account. If it turns out that we're to be here another year or two, I don't doubt that's what we will be doing."

There is not a great deal that I can add to this comprehensive summary of the way work and play have been administered with such success in maintaining the moral of the men of the Grand Fleet. The show in the "theatre ship" that night I found well worth the wet launch trip in a sloppy sea. It consisted of two parts of varieties and one of burlesque. Most of the numbers had been under rehearsal for several weeks, and the whole affair went off with all the aplomb of a London Revue. No "accessories"—from posters to programmes—were missing, not even the Censor.

An officer sitting next me, calling my attention to the blank back of the programme, said that he had written some "advertisements" to fill it, but that the Censor had banned them at the last moment as "not proper." As a matter of fact, there was far less in the whole show played by men to men, as it was, to "bring a blush to the cheek" than in the average West End Revue. A certain "chilliness" in the atmosphere of the auditorium, due to the fact that it was situated immediately over one of the refrigerating chambers, was more than neutralised by the warm reception the packed audience gave the show from the opening chorus to "God Save the King."

I managed to spend a few minutes at the nightly kinema show on several battleships. All of the available seats were invariably packed, with the enthusiasm tremendous, especially for the "knock-about" pictures. Charlie Chaplin appeared to be a ten-to-one favourite over any one else—both in the Ward Rooms and in the Lower Decks—and the demand for films in which he figured was a good deal greater than the available supply. The "sentimental" Mary Pickford sort of films were rather more popular than the men cared to show by their applause, but the harrowing "suffering-mother-and-child" subjects they would have none of. A rather poor film of Rider Haggard's *She* which I saw was very coldly received by both men and officers. The Official War films of all of the Allies were always sure of a rousing reception. A special treat was the picture of the King's recent visit to the Grand Fleet, which offered men and officers the exciting sport of "finding" themselves on various sectors of it. Travel films were in little demand, the reason for which was perhaps supplied by one of my "coaling-mates," who said that the only kind of travel "movie" that he was interested in was the woods of Scotland running north at sixty miles an hour past the window of his homebound train.

Besides the more or less organised forms of work and play, many of the men in the Fleet have some sort of a hobby to which they turn in the rare intervals which might otherwise be spent in "thumb-twirling" and "thinking," those twin enemies of "The Contented Sailor." Thousands of men "make things"—not the old ship-in-a-bottle seaside bar ornament sort, but objects of real usefulness. One officer had become a specialist on electrical heating contrivances, and had equipped the wardroom with cigar-lighters to work with the ship's "juice" and save matches. Another was making his own golf clubs, and I heard of a Captain of Royal Marines of noble lineage who had fabricated a very "wearable" pair of Norwegian ski-boots. There are so many skilled artisans among the men that one is not surprised to see them making almost anything; nevertheless, the gunner of one of the battleships who—with the sole exception of the lens—made a complete kinema projecting machine, did a very creditable piece of work.

Some of the senior Naval Officers have gone in for stock-breeding, overflowing to the land in their endeavours to find room to expand. Pig-raising is the most popular line, and there is great rivalry between the several "sty proprietors." A certain distinguished sailor—his name is a byword to the English people—discoursed learnedly to me for fifteen minutes on the strategy of the Battle of Jutland, and then, turning to a visiting officer, spoke with equal facility, and even greater enthusiasm, of his success in crossing the "China Poland" with the "Ordinary Orkney" to increase (or was it to reduce?) the "streak" in the bacon.

He called the new breed the "Chinorkland," or something like that, and if the fact that he was planning three or four generations ahead conveys anything as to the view the Navy takes regarding the duration of the war, my readers—with the Censor's indulgence—are welcome to the tip.

THE HEALTH OF THE FLEET

It was a great day for the Principal Medical Officer. In spite of the fact that there were nearer 1200 than 1100 men in his ship, the returns of "Sick" and "Hospital" cases had been recorded by successive "pairs of spectacles" for several days. Even a single twenty-four hours like that for a battleship on active service was worthy of remark, and three or four days of it undoubtedly constituted a record for the British or any other Navy. That the clean sheet would be spread over a whole week was almost too much to hope for, even after the sixth day of the double duck's eggs had gone by. But now the morning of the seventh day had come, the last of a week in which there had been no case of sickness in a ship which carried one of the largest, if not *the* largest, complement of men in the British Navy. It was no wonder that the P.M.O.'s eyes were beaming, and that he shook hands all round with his Staff Assistants, for it was an achievement which might well stand as a record for many a year.

"Since you do not appear likely to be troubled with anything worse than a rush of congratulations to-day, sir," I said, after extending my own felicitations, "perhaps you'll have time to tell me how you've done it. I've heard fine tributes paid the R.N.M.S. by French, American, and Italian doctors who know something of it, but I was hardly prepared to find you starting a sort of Ponce de Leon 'Fountain of Perpetual Youth,' in the British Fleet."

The P.M.O. laughed.

"Making a health resort of a battleship, with your dressing stations under casemates and your sick bay all but under a turret, does seem a bit like reversing the saying about 'in the midst of life we are in death,'" he replied. "But the fact remains that this ship—the whole of the Grand Fleet indeed—is one of the most remarkable 'health resorts' the world has ever known. Not since the dawn of history has there been a large body of men with so small a percentage of bodily ills and ailments as that which mans the ships of the Grand Fleet at this moment. This is due to the absolutely unique conditions which prevail here, and our success in maintaining and improving the standard of health is principally due to making the most of those conditions.

"The health of any community—of any body or collection of human beings—depends primarily upon the natural salubrity of the region in which it is located and the extent to which it is isolated from those living under less favourable conditions. A city may be very healthy naturally, but if its inhabitants are subject to a constant influx of more or less infected transients from less healthy places its own standard must inevitably be lowered. Under normal conditions, a modern warship—either in port or at sea—is one of the healthiest places in the world, and such sickness as prevails there is almost always contracted ashore and carried—and often spread—aboard.

"With a Fleet that has its base near a large city, so that the men are in more or less constant contact with those ashore, the health of the former will very largely depend upon the extent to which that contact can be controlled. Between dock-hands, etc., coming aboard and the sailors going ashore, it is difficult under such circumstances to keep the men afloat much healthier than those on the land. It is only when there is comparatively complete isolation from large cities that it is possible to take full advantage of the ideal conditions for maintaining physical healthfulness at sea, and such conditions exist at the Northern Base to a degree never before equalled in Naval history. Our success here is merely the consequence of making the most of those unique conditions.

"On the score of bodily healthfulness, life as lived in the Grand Fleet has more favouring conditions, and fewer unfavouring ones, than that possible at any other point at which a considerable fleet has ever had its base. Indeed, I could go farther than that, and say that never has a large number of men, either afloat or ashore, had such an opportunity to maintain so high a standard of physical health. In the first place, wet, cold, and stormy though it is for much of the year, the climate is a salubrious and invigorating one for the physically sound man that the sailor must be before he finds his way into the Navy at all. Even ashore the population is notably robust.

"In the next place, the anchorage is isolated, but not too isolated. It strikes almost the ideal mean on this score. In the ordinary routine, there is practically no contact whatever between those afloat and the people ashore. If the men land at all it will be for a game of football, a cross-country run, road work or something of the sort, in the course of which nothing whatever is seen of the resident population. It is not practicable to give the men a long enough shore leave to allow them to visit a neighbouring town, where one sees rather less navy blue as a rule than in many an inland town in England. The steward doing his marketing is about the only regular human link between a ship and the land, and his contact with those on shore is not of a character likely to be dangerous. This leaves the fresh drafts and the men returning from leave as almost the only possible carriers of new infection. How those are looked after I will explain presently.

"Much more complete isolation than this is, of course, effected when a cruiser or a fleet of cruisers goes on an extended voyage or patrol, but in such a case the freedom from contact with shore is offset by the more arduous conditions of life, especially in the matter of diet. The great thing about the situation of Scapa is that its unique position makes it possible to eliminate most of the rigors of sea life without being exposed to the health dangers of harbour life. A ship here can be just as well victualled as at Portsmouth, so far as the men are concerned, while letters and newspapers six times a week are ample service on that score. As I have said, the conditions for keeping mind and body at their best are ideal, and give us a unique opportunity for establishing new health records for the Navy.

"Of the two main channels by which disease could come to us from the outside—returning leave men and new drafts—the latter is the more dangerous, and therefore the one the more closely watched. Generally speaking, the men get leave about every nine months, this more or less roughly coinciding with a period in which the ship is in dock for repairs. If during a man's leave there is a case of any infectious or contagious disease in the house where he has stayed, or if he has reason to believe that he may have been exposed to infection or contagion elsewhere, he is ordered to report that fact immediately upon his return to the ship, when we take such precautions as the circumstances seem to warrant to prevent trouble. His clothes are disinfected, and he is ordered to report for examination over a period of days varying with the disease to which there was risk of his having been exposed. This enables us to isolate him (should it be necessary) before he is in a condition in which he could pass on the disease to others. A useful check which we have upon a man who might neglect to report his possible exposure to disease during his leave is the law which requires medical officers in all parts of Great Britain to ascertain if any soldier or sailor on leave is living in any house where there is a case of infectious disease, and to report this fact to the proper authorities. In this way it may be that we learn a man has been exposed even before he returns to the ship.

"New drafts are watched equally closely. Some time before a man's arrival a health sheet is sent to me on which is indicated any disease which he may have had during his period of service, together with information as to whether or not he may have been exposed to anything infectious in the interval immediately before he is sent to us. Any treatment for minor chronic ailments which may be in progress is continued in the ship. A general disinfection of kit and a daily reporting for twenty-one days for examination makes it practically impossible for a new rating to bring disease to the Ship's Company.

"The greatest obstacle to the preservation of perfect health in the men on a warship is the unavoidable necessity of having them sleep close together in comparatively confined spaces. This ship, from the fact that she was originally designed for a foreign Power, is worse off than most modern battleships on that score, and, everything else equal, would be more difficult to keep the men in health in than in any of the others. This is one of the reasons why I am so gratified by our showing of the past week. Sleeping in hammocks in itself is not unhealthy—quite the contrary, in fact—but the danger lies in the chance an infectious disease has to spread among so many men lying almost side by side and head to feet. Thorough ventilation is the best preventive of disease under the circumstances; this has been provided by fans.

"The one thing dreaded above all others on a warship is cerebro-spinal meningitis, both on account of its unavoidably high rate of mortality and the difficulty of preventing its spread under the limiting conditions. Luckily, we have had practically none of it up here. In the event of the appearance of a case of any infectious disease, the man is isolated, the men of his mess are put under observation, and all of their clothes are disinfected. As soon as possible the case is removed to one of the hospital ships which are always here. The restricted sleeping quarters occasionally are responsible for the quick spread of a bad cold, but the fresh air, free from germs, makes anything like an epidemic of influenza almost out of the question in the Grand Fleet. German measles has been rather a nuisance once or twice; in fact, we have seen rather more of it than we have of the German Fleet. If the latter is as easily disposed of as the former, however, we shall have little to complain of."

Of the progressiveness and general up-to-dateness of the Royal Navy Medical Service, I had already heard from a number of sources (I remember in particular how Madame Carrel had told me that the British Admiralty had adopted the remarkable "irrigation" treatment, discovered and perfected by her distinguished husband, long before any French military hospital would even consider it), so I was quite prepared to find every ship in the Grand Fleet amply provided to handle "action eventualities."

The problems of a hospital on a warship are quite different from those of even an advanced hospital at the Front. The latter has a fluctuating but more or less unbroken stream of casualties to handle, with sometimes weeks of warning when defensive or offensive action will make unusual demands. A battleship may easily be lying quietly at anchor in the morning and be joined in a death-grapple in the evening. Her surgeons may have spent a year with nothing more to keep their hands in than reducing sprains and stitching up cuts, and then a hundred casualties may drop out of the sky in the wake of a single enemy salvo. For them, it rarely rains but it pours, though it may be a long time between the storms.

The usual practice is for a warship to have a small permanent sick bay and hospital capable of coping with routine exigencies, and to supplement these during and after action by converting certain favourably located parts of the ship—always below the water-line if possible—into action dressing-stations. The equipment of these latter—operating tables, beds, lights, etc.—is all made on collapsible lines and kept stored close at hand. The battleship whose remarkable health record I am writing about, takes especial pride in the fact that it has two action dressing-stations, permanently equipped and ready for use at a moment's notice.

The men in the various turrets and casemates, as well as in all other parts of the ship where casualties are likely to occur in action, are trained to give first aid and carry their wounded to the nearest dressing-station. For the latter purpose a specially designed stretcher is used, so constructed that the wounded men, strapped in securely, can be carried at any angle with a minimum of discomfort. The stretcher at present in use in the British Navy is of Japanese manufacture. It is made almost entirely of canvas and strips of bamboo, the two materials which experience has shown are the best combination on the score of lightness and strength.

As soon as possible after an action the badly wounded are transferred to a base hospital ship, whence, as soon as they are able to stand the voyage, they are sent in a carrier ship to one of the big R.N.M.S. hospitals.

The superlative care which has been taken of the bodily health of the men of the Grand Fleet has been one of the main, if not *the* main factor in contributing to the healthiness of mind and the keenness of spirit which have made it possible for them to "stick out" their long vigil in the northern seas.

ECONOMY IN THE GRAND FLEET

The wind had been whistling raw and cold through the foretop, from where I had been watching the night target practice, and my appetite was whetted to a razor edge by the time the game was over and the ship was again at anchor.

"I'm as hungry as a shark myself," said the Gunnery Commander, "but never mind, we'll have a good snack of supper just as soon as we climb down and get out of these Arctic togs."

Five minutes later, the first of a dozen officers who stamped in as fast as their duties were over, we were seated at one of the wardroom tables. "Would you rather have ham or sardine sandwiches?" some one asked. "Both!" I unblushingly replied, "unless the sardines are as large as whales."

A waiter came hurrying through the door in answer to the ring, buttoning his coat as though he had been surprised by an unexpected summons. "A couple of plates of ham and sardine sandwiches and beer all round," was the laconic but comprehensive order.

The old "Marine" smiled deprecatingly, as one who has unpleasant news to impart. "Sorry, sir," he said, addressing the Commander, "but the day's bread was finished at dinner, sir, an' the 'am we 'ad for breakfast was all we can 'ave to-day, sir."

And then the wonderful thing happened. I had expected the howl of a Roman stage mob to greet the disappointing announcement, but it was only the Commander's voice that was heard, speaking quietly as he rose from the table. "Very well, Jenkins," he said; "bring us some hot cocoa in the smoking-room. A good hot drink's the best thing for a night like this anyway."

Over steaming cups of the most nutritious and sustaining of drinks, the Commander told me, quite briefly and casually, something of what had been done in his ship (which was thoroughly typical of the other units of the Grand Fleet) to cut down the unnecessary consumption of food.

"The old idea," he said, "that a fighting man ought to be stuffed like a prize steer was discredited by experience long ago, but it took the war to jar us into putting that experience (like so many other things) into practice. Any man living a non-sedentary life will make a very brave attempt to eat all the food that is put before him, but that by no means proves that he needs it. If he is working hard enough in the open air the surplus over his normal requirement doesn't do him any harm, and so there wasn't much point in keeping it away from him as long as there was food to waste all over the world. But when the world's surplus began to be turned into a deficit by the war, the opportunity arose to kill two birds with one stone—to save food and to improve the health of the men. I am glad to say that we have been able to do both, and that, moreover, with the hearty concurrence of every one concerned, both officers and men. It's the same kind of thing that could be done with the civil population if only they were subject to the same control as the Navy. Perhaps, if an adequate rationing scheme can be devised, this will be accomplished.

"Generally speaking," he continued, "we have left the Navy ration just about as it was before the war, with the exception of those staples in which there is the worst shortage—bread, meat, and potatoes. The latter could be relaxed now if we desired, as there is ample supply in sight; but—to save transport and because we are better off anyhow on our present ration—even that item will probably remain as it is. Indeed, great as the actual food-saving has been, a still more important benefit has been that to our health. There are several factors contributing to the fact that the personnel of the Grand Fleet has incomparably the highest standard of health ever maintained in so large a body of men, and I am quite positive that by no means the least of these is the check that has been put on overeating by our food-saving measures. Again, I am sure that the civil population would be equally benefited by similar restriction."

This incident occurred on the occasion of my first visit to the Grand Fleet in the late fall of last year, but it was not until my return nearly two months later that I had opportunity to gather anything further of the details of food economy. Then I learned that a strict rationing was only the first part of a scheme of which the second was a waste prevention campaign. Bread and meat were both further restricted, but to the improvement rather than the detriment of the already high health standard of the Fleet. The bread now served consists of one-eighth potato, one-sixth barley meal, and the remainder—but slightly more than two-thirds—of "standard" flour, which itself contains a high percentage of the whole wheat. The Fleet Paymaster of my ship, who outlined the scheme to me, said that the idea was to reduce waste to a minimum, both "coming" and "going." "We aim to put no more food on the tables of either the officers or men than they will eat up clean. 'Jack Spratt' and his wife are our models. We try to see that the 'platter' is 'licked clean.' But we don't stop there by any means. 'Jack Spratt,' so far as we have any information, must have thrown away the bones, even if he and the missus did lick the platter. We not only save the bones, but even go so far as to skim the grease off the dish-water the platter is washed in. If you'll run over this report here you'll understand the 'fade-away' expression on the faces of the gulls that used to fatten on the waste of the

Grand Fleet. It is merely a tabulated summary of a week's saving of the things which used to go down the chutes for the birds and the fishes."

There were numbers running to four and five figures in the table, most of them referring to the pounds of various refuse which had been collected and shipped for conversion into glycerine and other useful and valuable products. Without giving figures which might be "useful or heartening to the enemy," I will probably be permitted to state that the various headings were the following: Drippings, Fat Meat, Bones, Waste Paper, Bottles and Jars, Discarded Clothing, Lead Seals, Mail Bags and Tins. Several of the items would have run to substantial figures even in tons, and the money received for them at even the nominal prices paid by the contractor aggregated many thousands of pounds.

"You will now understand," continued the Fleet Paymaster, "just how it made us feel when we read in a London paper a few days ago a statement to the effect that *if* the Navy had gone in for waste-saving in the same way the Army had, a certain total would have been greatly increased. Since we've been going into this sort of thing heart and soul for more than a year, and since it is far easier to check waste on a ship (where you have absolute control of all the in-comings and out-goings) than on land, you can imagine that reading that sort of 'tosh' makes us feel—well, about as we do when we try to digest the wisdom of the 'Naval Strategic Writers' of the type that want to put the Grand Fleet on wheels and send it to Berlin." Glancing quickly through the figures under the headings opposite the various ships of our squadron I noticed at once that there were considerable variations in their savings, and, knowing that the number of men did not vary materially on any of them, I asked the reason why the Flagship, for instance, with less than half the weight of "Bones" to her credit than "Ourself," was still able to put by something like 50 per cent. more "Drippings."

"It will probably be because we haven't yet 'standardized' our methods throughout the Fleet," replied the Paymaster; "because different ships may have different ways of going about the job. Of these particular items you have mentioned, perhaps we can find out something by talking to Mr. C——, the Warrant Officer who has charge of the collection of by-products."

Mr. C——, who was plainly an enthusiast, launched into the subject with eagerness.

"I've been intending to explain that matter of the drippings to you, sir," he said, addressing the Fleet Paymaster, "for the figures certainly have the look of not doing us justice. Fact is, though, that the only reason we've run behind the Flagship on this count is because I have been encouraging the messes to carry food-saving one stage farther by using the clean grease— the skimmings from their soup and the water their meat is boiled in—

instead of margarine. With a little pepper and salt, most of them like it better even than butter, and of course they can use it much more free. And since dripping is worth much more for food than it ever can be to make up into soap or explosives, I figure I'm on the right track, even if it does give the *Lucifer* and the *Mephistopheles* a chance to head us in the 'grease' column. I must admit though, sir, that they've both been gaining a few pounds of second quality stuff by rigging 'traps'—settling tubs at the bottoms of their chutes—in which they catch any grease that has got away from them in the galley. I'll be beating them at that game before long, though, for I'm putting in settling tubs at both top and bottom, with a strainer in between.

"As for the 'Bones,'" he went on, turning to me, "that's largely 'personality.' 'Boney Joe,' my chief assistant, is perhaps more largely responsible than any one else for the fact that we are not only the champion 'bone-collecting' ship of the squadron, but also head the list with 'Bottles and Jars' and 'Empty Tins.' With 'Waste Paper' there's no use competing with the Flagships, for they come in for an even heavier bombardment of that kind of stuff from the Admiralty than we do; and as for 'Discarded Clothing,' I feel that a place at the bottom of the column would be more likely to indicate economical management than one at the top. But the things that represent a sheer saving, the things that used to be thrown away right along—they're what it's worth while piling up by every means we can, and they're the ones I want to keep heading the columns with. And, as I said before, 'Boney Joe' is the main feature of the show on this score. If you like, I will arrange it so that you can do his morning round with him to-morrow."

I accepted the offer with alacrity, for I had heard, or heard of, "Boney Joe" on several occasions already, but without once getting my eyes on him. The first time was when, in order to avoid a howling blizzard which was raging outside, I endeavoured to make my way forward to the ladders leading up to my cabin under the bridge by threading the mazes of the mess deck. Bent almost double to keep from butting the low swung hammocks, I tripped the more easily over a box of empty tins, and fell with one arm sousing elbow-deep into what proved to be a tub of "frozen" grease. Surveying the draggled cuff of my jacket in the morning, my servant pronounced his verdict without a moment's hesitation.

"'Tumblin' into 'Boney Joe's' pickin's last night, sir, was you?" he said with a grin; "we's allus doin' it oursel's."

On a number of other occasions certain sirenical notes which came floating up to my cabin from the mess deck were variously ascribed to "'Boney Joe' doin' 'is rounds," "'Boney Joe' cadgin' for grease," and "Boney Joe singin' 'is 'Mornin' 'Ate.'" I had several pictures of "Boney Joe" in my mind, but not one of them came near to fitting the handsome, strongly built and thoroughly sailorly man-o'-war's-man whom Mr. C—— introduced to me as the bearer of that storied name on the following morning. Only a sort of scallawag twinkle in his eye revealed him as a man who liked his little joke.

"If you don't mind, sir," he said, saluting, "we'll clean up these last two flats, an' then we'll be clear to push along up to my 'bonatorium' an' have a bit o' a yarn."

Working with neatness and dispatch, "Joe" and his half-dozen assistants made rapid progress with their clean-up. "Pick-uppy" as the job was, everything was really in admirable order. Bones, papers, tins, bottles and grease—each had its separate receptacle. The grease was already hardening in large cans: the other refuse was in boxes or tubs. In each mess was one small tub with a few sad bits of assorted food in the bottom. Unable to classify this, I asked "Joe" what orphan asylum these crumbs were intended for.

"Not for no orphan 'sylum, sir," he replied with an appreciative grin; "only for the piggery. We don't keep no pigs oursel's, sir, but the A'miral on the 'X. Y. Z.' does, an' we all 'elps wi' wot we kin spare. They sends round a drifter tu pick up the leavin's ev'ry day or two, but Lor' bless yu', ther' ain't no leavin's since we got our by-producks macheen a-workin'. If the rest o' the ships don't dish out no more pig feed an' what we does, the 'X. Y. Z.'s' live stock'll be gettin' so thin they'll blow away one o' these days. This ain't really no place fer pigs and gulls no more, sir."

Considerable as the accumulation was, it was loosely sacked in a few minutes, after which it was carried forward to the hold where the repacking for shipment was carried on. This consisted largely of protecting the bottles with straw, forcing small tins inside of large ones, pouring the grease into larger cans and putting the bones into stronger sacks. "Joe" said that he called the place his "bonatorium" partly because bones formed the largest and most valuable item of shipment, but principally because they were his "favrut produck," the one he took the most pride in collecting. Even the few days' accumulation of refuse on hand was of huge bulk. I saw at once how important a work was being carried on, and had no envy for the pig or the gull whose lot it was to live on what is now thrown away by the Grand Fleet.

Mr. C—— was called away at this juncture, and, left cock of his own dunghill, "Boney Joe" became at once his own natural self. The sailorly man-o'-war's-man disappeared in an instant, and only one of the drollest characters in the British Navy remained behind.

"I'll be showin' yu 'ow I goes out tu drum up me bone trade," he said, throwing an empty sack over his shoulder and replacing his beribboned cap with a crumpled velour of the Hombourg type. "Found it in me pickin's; spose it kum from one o' the orficers," he added parenthetically, giving the queer headpiece a proprietary pat with his free hand. "Now 'ere's wot I sing tu 'em. Made it up mysel', too."

With a quick double-shuffle he began footing it up and down the junk-cluttered deck of the "bonatorium," singing in a voice which cut the air like the whine of the wind through the radio aerials.

"'Eave out all yer dead an' dyin','Eave out all yer bones an' fat,'Eave out the stiff o' 'Littl' Willie,'An' I'll give yu my 'at."

"Course I don't reely give 'em the 'at, sir," explained the singer, stopping for a moment in his march. "Th' 'at's only bait. But, jest th' same, they 'eaves out the bones an' fat all right. Last night they 'eaved a bone jest back o' me ear. Safest way's fer four o' us tu form a holler square an' so pertect the flanks, so tu speak. Nother thing. Yu 'eard me sing "Eave out "Littl' Willie"' jest now? Wull, most times I sings it "Eave out th' Kaisur's dotter,' meanin' Queen Sophy o' Greece, cose she's a rum un fer fair. But knowin' that in th' wardroom it warn't th' custim tu menshun a lydy's nyme in publick like, I brings in Willie insted."

"But why celebrate the young Hohenzollern in song at all?" I asked in perplexity. "I don't quite trace the connexion between the 'dead and dying,' and 'bones and fat' and the—the earthly remains of 'Little Willie.'"

"I ain't celebratin' 'em," explained "Joe"; "I'm abominatin' 'em, so tu speak. My refrunce is tu the dead an' dyin' sojers th' Kaisur cooks up tu make glysreen frum. I brings in Sophy an' Willie jest tu make 'em feel how they'd like it if 'twas their turn next."

Having cleared up this point, "Joe" began to shuffle again. "Nother thing I sing 'em is th' follerin'," he said.

"'Eave out all yure bones, bottles, tins, fats, boots and shoes,If yu don't 'eave out you'll be sure to lose—Cose then I'll pinch th' 'ull blinkin' lot mesel'!"

"An' tyke it frum me, I does pinch 'em too," he added, stopping in front of me again. "Likewise, any other reefoose—like ov'ralls an' such left lyin' roun' wher' it 'adn't ought tu be. Sum times they gets 'em back, an' sum times they duzen't. Serves 'em jolly well rite for bein' keerless."

At this juncture I began to search my pockets for a piece of paper upon which to jot down the burden of "Joe's" cries.

"Never mind, sir," he said cheerily as my hands came up empty, "ther's allus whatev'r yure needin' in th' stayshunary line in my wastepaper dupartment."

He threw back the cover of a huge box, and at almost the first grab brought up a scented sheet of pink note paper which—except where some one had written "Dear Kitty—Just a line to tell you I am in the pink and hoping——" followed by a blot, and a grease-spot in the middle—was just as good as new.

"This dupartment is both my joy an' my sorrer," said "Joe" pensively, digging his arm deep into the soft depths. "I salves the story o' 'Arseen Lupin' an' a Gieves joolry catalog—both compleet—this mornin', an' I've laid by some 'Merican papers (Pittsburg, I b'leeve) fer yu, sir. But th' tantylysin thing about it is what's allus missin'. Jest look at this, fer instance, sir," and he fished a greasy fragment of paper from a pocket of his overall and handed it to me. In a highly appropriate "atmosphere"—with the scent of fat to starboard, the fragrance of bones to port, and the ineffable odours of the "crumbs" grudgingly allotted to the "X. Y. Z.'s" piggery rising from the depths of the tub on the rim of which I sat—I read the following, just this and no word more:—

A SWEET SMELLING SAVOUR

I

Some rave about the subtle scents of Araby and Ind,Of camphor and of ambergris, of sandal-wood and musk,The poet chants the praises of the violet and the rose,And stately lilies standing by the dew-drenched lawn at dusk.

II

My lady loves the lavender with, slender ...The lover loves whatever perfume ...The cow-slips simple fragrance ...The pine-wood's spicy ...

III

But, far beyond all ...The smell of ...

"It fair to druv me crazy huntin' fer that missin' peece," said "Joe" with a hurt sort of "'twas-ever-thus" expression in his eyes; "an' I felt it espeshul, sir, becus I writes po'try and songs a bit mysel'. 'E was jest workin' up tu a climacks, an' I'm wonderin' all th' time what it wuz that smelt better'n 'ambygris' an' musk an' roses an' lilies an' all the rest. D'yu spose, sir, it cud a bin that stuff they put in brilyantin?" and he ran stubby fingers through his hair in an apparent endeavour to waft me a whiff of the odour which had been there the Sunday before the last coaling.

A frivolous impulse prompted me to bid him ask the "X. Y. Z.'s" pigs, but the look in his eyes sobered me, and I said I felt sure it must have been "Attar of Roses," as that was said to be the most expensive of all perfumes.

"Joe" returned the fragment to his pocket, a brooding shadow sitting on his brow. "Ther' wuz only one thing ever fussed me more'n not locatin' th' end o' that pome, sir," he said sadly, beginning to fumble anew, "and that wuz this."

The greasy fragment which he unfolded and handed to me barely hung together at the blackened creases, but—well, no one who has ever watched wardroom firelight throw its rosy glow over the pinky pages of *La Vie Parisienne* will ever fail to recognise the flimsiest wisp of it blowing before a winter gale.

"That's th' wrong side, sir," said "Joe," as I took the sheet tenderly and began to puzzle my way through a chart which was averred to be some sort of barometer of the emotions. "Scuse me, sir, but this is th' way. No, not like that. You've got 'er upside down. Ther', *that's* 'er, or ruther wot's left o' 'er. Now wot d'yu think o' that fer tough luck?"

It had been just the usual *La Vie* picture, nothing more or nothing less. A frou-frou of *lingerie*, a flash or two of pink cuticle, and—the rest was torn away.

"Wot makes it 'arder tu bear," said "Joe" mournfully, "is th' fack that it ain't offen that th' orficers let th' pictur' pages drift this far forrard th' wardroom. I 'ad picked up th' 'parly-voo' pages offen enuf, but a pictur', nary a one. An' now w'en this one comes, it's ripped off jest when it 'gins tu get good. Spose sum orficer, tryin' tu save matches, used th' best o' 'er tu lite 'is pipe wi."

I think that I did quite the kindest thing possible under the circumstances when I patted "Joe" sympathetically on the shoulder and assured him that, so far as my not inconsiderable experience with *La Vie* pictures went, there was nothing to indicate that this one "got any better" on the missing fragment, and that I felt quite confident that "th' best o' 'er" had *not* gone to light an "orficer's pipe."

Apparently a good deal cheered, "Joe" returned lightsomely to "shop," and told me with much gusto of a great find he had had that morning in the shape of an "'arf pound o' solid beef" hidden away in the angle of a bone. His first impulse, he said, had been to report the careless cook to the Fleet Paymaster, but on second thought he had decided to say nothing and contribute the morsel as "extra ration" to his mess.

"That way," he said philosophically, "I'll stop th' waste jest the same, an' yet won't start a ructshun wi' one o' me colleegs that mite throw me collectin' macheenry out o' order. Nuthin' like cuttin' down fricshun in this 'ere econ'my game."

There is a "Boney Joe" on every ship of the British Navy to-day. Could we not do with a few more of him in civil life as the time draws near when the hope of victory rests more and more on personal economy and universal saving?

CHRISTMAS IN A "HAPPY" SHIP

There was a hint of Christmas in the long stacks of parcels mail on the station platform and the motley array of packages in the hands of the waiting sailors, but for the rest there was nothing to differentiate the "Fleetward"-bound train from the same train as one might have seen it on any other day of the year. There is only a certain small irreducible minimum of men which can be spared from a fighting ship which at any time is liable to be sent into action, and the season sacred to the Prince of Peace is no exception.

To the average land-lubber nothing could appear nearer to the height of misfortune than the lot of the sailor who has to leave a nice, warm, comfortable hearthside in the south of England and return to his unceasing vigil in the storm-tossed northern seas at the one time of year set apart above all others for the family and the home, and I did my best to introduce a note of sympathy into my voice when I tried to condole with the ruddy-faced man-o'-war's man who had kindly volunteered to help me find my compartment.

"'Ard to be goin' back abord on Crismus Day, you think, sir?" he asked with a grin. "P'haps it is jest a bit 'ard to leave the missus jest now, but—ther' ain't no qu'ues in Scarpa Flow, and I've got a jolly good lot o' mates waitin' fer me in the ol' ———. She's a happy ship if ther' ever wuz un, an' Crismus at sea ain't 'arf so bad as you mite think, sir."

That there were several hundred similar-minded philosophers travelling by that train became evident at a point where they met and mingled for a space with some of the "lucky" ones who were gathering there to go home on a leave which had providentially coincided with the holiday season. Scan as closely as I would the men in the long blue lines, there was nothing to distinguish the "returning from" to the "going on" save the fact that the former were bulging with Christmas parcels.

Nor was there about any of the officers I met in the course of my northward journey any suggestion of an air of martyrdom on account of the fact that it was their lot to spend Christmas afloat instead of ashore. One of them was going to join a Destroyer Flotilla leader, and was too busy congratulating himself on the fact that he was to be second to a commander who had the reputation of having a "nose for trouble," and the faculty of always being "among those present" when anything of interest occurred in the North Sea to have time to lament the fact that he was missing—this time by only a couple of days—his eighth consecutive Christmas with his family. Another had equally high hopes of the life of adventure which awaited him in the light cruiser he had been appointed to, and a third entertained me for an hour with yarns of wardroom pranks on a battleship to which he was returning after a special course in gunnery at a south-coast port. It was the latter who used the identical expression in describing his ship as had been employed by the sailor I have quoted above.

"She's a happy ship, is the old ———," he said with an affectionate smile, "and it's glad I am to be getting back to her again."

The only man I met on the whole journey who seemed in the least sorry for himself was a King's Messenger—he was carrying a turkey under one arm and a dispatch box under the other—who complained that his schedule would not take him back to London until Christmas afternoon.

In the battleship to which I reported about the only evidence of Yule-tide observable on my arrival was the huge accumulation of "homebound" letters which the wardroom officers were engaged in censoring. The day before Christmas was distinctly "routine," with just a suggestion of festivity beginning to become manifest towards evening. The loungers by the wardroom fire smoked, chatted, and read the paper for an hour after dinner was over, but showed no disposition to melt away to bed as in the usual order of things. About ten o'clock a violin, banjo, and a one-stringed fiddle with a brass horn attached made their appearance, and upon these never entirely harmonising instruments their owners began inconsequentially to strum and scrape. As fragments of familiar airs became faintly recognisable, the loungers began to lay aside papers and cigars and to join in the choruses in that half-furtive manner so characteristic of the Briton in his first fore-running essays at "close harmony." Until he is assured of the vocal support of his neighbour, there is no sound in the world—from the roar of the lion to the roar of the cannon—which the average Englishman dreads so much as that of his own voice raised in song.

Volume increased with confidence, and it was not many minutes before the choruses were booming at full blast. For a while it was the more popular numbers from the late London revues which had the call, but these soon gave way to ragtime, and that in turn to those old familiar songs which have warmed the hearts and bound closer the ties of comradeship of the good fellows of the Anglo-Saxon world since ships first began to set sail from the shores of England to people the ends of the earth. From "Clementine" and "Who Killed Cock Robin?" to "Swanee River," and "My Old Kentucky Home," there was not a song that I had not heard—and even boomed raucously away in the choruses of myself—a hundred times in all parts of America. Every one of them is in the old "College Song Book," not a one of them, but which every man of the millions America is training for the Great Fight could have joined in without faking a word or a note.

A slight shifting of the gilt braid on the blue sleeves, a reshuffling of the papers and magazines on the table, and the wardroom of the —— might have passed for that of any American battleship. The interposing of four poster and pennant peppered walls, the placing of the lounging figures in proper mufti, and you would have had a room in an American college "frat house" or club. The men, the songs, the vibrant spirit of good fellowship would have done for either of the settings.

Poignantly suggestive of the things of bygone college days was the change which came over the spirit of the scene when an exuberant young sub-lieutenant began doing stunts by trying to climb round a service chair without touching the deck. His inevitable fall upset the tilted chair of a visiting "snotty," who was playing his mandolin, and an instant later the two were rolling in a close embrace. Suddenly some one shouted "scrum!" and with an impetuous rush the singers ranged themselves into two rival "Rugger" teams, each trying to push the other against the wall.

Twitching at the stir of long dormant impulses, I restrained myself with an effort from mixing in the joyous mêlée, and maintained my dignity as a newly arrived visitor by backing into a corner and erecting a sofa barricade against the swirling human tide.

"Shades of Stanford and old Encina Hall" (I found myself gasping), "it's a 'rough-house,' a real college 'rough-house.'"

While it lasted that "scrum" had all the fierce abandon of a Freshman-Sophomore "cane rush," but even at its very climax (when it had upset the electric heater and was threatening to engulf the coal stove) there was a differentiation. One sensed rather than saw the thread of control restraining it, and knew that every pushing, laughing player of the game was subconsciously alert for a signal that would send him, tense and ready, to the performance of those complexly simple duties training for which he had given the best part of his life.

"Rugger" gave place to "chair polo," and that highly diverting sport in turn to comparatively "formal" bouts of wrestling and feats of strength and agility. It was while a row of shirt-sleeved figures were at the height of a "bat" competition (which consisted of seeing which one could hang the longest by his toes from a steel beam of the ceiling) that the Fleet Surgeon edged gingerly in behind my barrier and remarked that it was "funny to think how that up-ended line of young fighting cocks might be tumbling from their roost to go to action stations at the next tick of the clock. And they'd fight just like they play," he went on, fingering a sprained wrist that was proffered for diagnosis. "We've not a single case of any kind in the hospital to-day, and the men are just as healthy in mind as they are in body. It's half the battle, let me tell you, to live in a happy ship."

Christmas morning broke cold and clear, with a roystering wind from the north furrowing the Flow with translucent ridges of white-capped jade and chrysoprase. All but the imperative routine duties of the ship were suspended, and the men spent many hours decorating the mess deck for their midday feast. When all was ready the band, its various members masquerading as everything from Red Cross nurses and ballet girls to German naval prisoners and American cowboys, came to lead the Captain and wardroom officers on their ceremonial Christmas visiting round. From mess to mess we marched, the capering band leading the way and a policeman with a "sausage" club shepherding the stragglers at the rear. Every table was loaded not only with its Christmas dinner, but also with all the gifts received by those who sat there, as well as with any trinkets or souvenirs they had picked up in the course of their foreign cruises. Especially and intentionally conspicuous were numerous home photographs, stuck up in or propped against the cakes and boxes of sweets. Most of the tables had "Merry Christmas" and various other seasonal mottoes printed with letters ingeniously built from cigarettes.

A running fire of greeting met us at every turn, and at each table cigarettes, sweets, or chunks of succulent plum pudding were pressed upon us. Acceptance for the most part was on the ancient "touch and remit" system. I noticed that the officers spoke to most of the men directly under them by name, and that the exchange of greetings was invariably of unfeigned cordiality on both sides. The tour completed, the band escorted us aft, where, with a hearty three cheers and a "tiger" for the Captain and Commander severally, and the wardroom officers jointly, it left us and rollicked back to serenade the feasters forward.

Christmas chapel was a simple Church of England service without a sermon, followed by Holy Communion for those who desired to celebrate it. Luncheon, in order that the wardroom servants could be free for feasting with their mates, was on the buffet plan, each officer serving himself from a side table.

Two or three of the men with whom I had spoken in the course of the morning round, had used that now familiar expression about the good fortune of being in a "happy" ship, but the climax was capped that evening at dinner (at which the wardroom entertained the Warrant Officers) when the Captain employed it in explaining the easy *bonne camaraderie* characterising that interesting occasion. I had told him how many times I had heard the words in question since my arrival, and asked him point blank if I was to assume by implication that the other ships of the Fleet were only dismal prisons of steel in comparison.

"Perhaps the men would try to make you believe something to that effect," he laughed, "but so also would those of the '——,' and the '——,' and the '——' regarding each other, the rest of the squadron and the whole of the Grand Fleet. As a matter of fact, if you had been on any one of them during the last twenty-four hours, you would probably have seen and heard and experienced just about what you have seen and heard and experienced here. You will not go far wrong if you say we are all 'Happy Ships' up here. The 'Happy Ship' is a tradition of the British Navy, and it's the one type of craft which does not become out of date with the march of science and the passage of the years."

IN A BALLOON SHIP

I had crossed in the old *Xerxes* in those ancient days when, as the latest launched greyhound of the Cunarder fleet, she held for a few precarious months the constantly shifting blue-ribbon for the swiftest transatlantic passage; but in that angular "cubistic" lump of lead-grey looming over the bow of my spray-smothered launch to blot out the undulant skyline of the nearest Orkney, there was not one familiar feature. Her forward funnel had been "kippered" down the middle to somewhere about on the level of the lower deck, and carried up in two smaller stacks which rose abreast to port and starboard. This had been done (as I learned later) to make room for a platform leading forward from the waist over which seaplanes could be wheeled to the launching-stage, which ran out over the bow from beneath the bridge. The break in the forecastle had been closed in connexion with a sweeping alteration which had converted the whole forward end of the main deck into a roomy seaplane "repository" and repair shop.

The changes aft were no less startling. The old poop seemed to have been razed to extend the last two hundred feet of the main deck, and over the ten or fifteen-feet-high railing, which surrounded this, the top of a partly inflated observation balloon showed like the back of a half-submerged turtle. The whole effect was weird and "impossible" in the extreme, and I felt like exclaiming with the yokel who saw a giraffe for the first time: "Aw, there ain't no such animal."

I had been asked aboard the *Xerxes* for an afternoon of seaplane and balloon practice. I had already seen a good deal of the former at various points in the Mediterranean and Adriatic, but the towed observation balloon—the "kite," as they call it—was an entirely new thing. I "put in" at once for an ascent in a kite, for I was anxious not only to get some sort of a firsthand idea of how it was being employed against submarines—of which I had already heard not a little—and also to compare the work with that of handling the ordinary observation balloons, of which I had seen so much in France, Italy, and the Balkans. The captain—whom I found just getting the ship under weigh from the bridge—after some hesitation, promised to "see what he could do," if there was not too much wind, when he was ready for "balloon work."

To one who has had experience only of hangars on land, perhaps the most impressive thing about an "aeroship" is the amount of gear and equipment which can be stowed and handled in restricted spaces. Wings and rudders which fold and refold upon each other until they form compact bundles that can be trundled about by a man or two, collapsible fuselages and pontoons, wheels which detach at a touch of a lever, "knock-down" transmissions—these things were everywhere the rule. One "baby" scout I saw almost completely assembled on the launching-stage, and the "tail," which a couple of men wired to the main body in a little more than a minute, I would have sworn I could have knocked off with a single well-placed kick. Yet, five minutes later, I saw that same machine "loop," "side-flop," "double-bank," and (quite at the will of its young pilot, who is rated the most expert seaplane man in the British Naval Air Service) recover at the end of a five-hundred-feet rolling fall, all without apparently starting a strut or rivet. "Collapsibility" and portability are evidently secured without sacrificing any essential strength.

The science of working the seaplane from the deck of a ship is still in process of development. Even up to quite recently it was the practice to put a machine overboard on a sling, and allow it to start from the water. The use of detachable wheels—which fall off into the sea after they have served their purpose in giving the preliminary run—has made launching from the deck practicable and comparatively safe, but the problem of landing even a wheeled machine on deck has not yet been satisfactorily solved. On account of lack of room, most of the experiments in this direction have ended disastrously, even tragically.

When a seaplane is about to be launched, after the usual preliminary "tuning" up on the launching-stage, the ship is swung dead into the teeth of the wind and put at full speed. This matter of wind direction is very important, for its variation by a fraction of a point from "head-on" may easily make a crooked run and a fluky launching. As the latter would almost inevitably mean that both plane and pilot must be churned under the swiftly advancing fore-foot of the ship, no precautions calculated to avoid it are omitted. Besides a wind-pennant at one end of the bridge, assurance is made doubly sure by the turning on of a jet of steam in the mathematical centre of the extreme tip of the launching-stage. When the back-blown steam streams straight along the middle plank of the stage, the wind is "right."

The captain, from the bridge, lifts a small white flag as a signal to the wing-commander that all is ready. The latter nods to the pilot, who starts his engine at full speed, while two mechanicians, braced against cleats on the deck, hold back the tugging seaplane. If the "tone" of the engine is right, the wing-commander (standing in front of the plane, and a little to one side) brings down his red-and-yellow flag, with a sharp jerk, falls on his face to avoid a collision, and the machine, freed from the grip of the men holding it, jumps away. The next two seconds tell the tale, for if a seaplane "gets off the deck" properly, the rest of its flight is not likely to be "eventful."

At practice, a seaplane sails over and drops its detachable wheels near a waiting drifter, which picks them up and returns them to the ship. The machine swoops low, and "kicks" loose the "spares" at a hundred feet or less above the surface of the water, and a pilot who let his wheels go from a considerably greater altitude drew a growl from the bridge, as a long fall is likely to injure them. Its flight over, a seaplane returns to the ship by alighting on the water several hundred yards astern, and floundering up alongside as best it can. With a high wind and a choppy sea, it is rough work. The machine is so "balanced" that its tractor propeller should revolve in the air and clear the water by several inches, even in a rough sea. It will occasionally strike into "green water," however, which is always likely to shatter the ends of the blades, if nothing else. The sheathing of the blades with metal affords considerable protection, though a certain risk is always present. The operation of picking a seaplane up and hoisting it inboard is a nice piece of seamanship at best, but in bad weather is a practicable impossibility. With a wind much above thirty miles an hour, indeed, only a very real need is likely to induce a "mother ship" to loose her birds from the home nest. With a sea too rough to make it possible for a seaplane to live in it, it is sometimes possible to carry on imperative reconnaisance by sending up an ordinary aeroplane (some of which are always carried); though the latter must, of course, make its landing on *terra firma* when its work is over.

The wind had been freshening considerably all afternoon, but with no more than thirty miles an hour showing on the indicator, there was no reason for not letting me have my "balloon ride."

As the time approached for its ascent, the balloon was allowed to rise far enough from the deck to permit its car to be pushed underneath the centre of it, in order that the latter might not be dragged in the "getaway." I could now see that the monster had rather the form of the "bag" of an airship than the "silkworm-with-stomach-cramps" shape of the regulation modern observation balloon. Its nose was less blunt than that of the "sausage," and the ropes were attached so that it would be pulled with that nose boring straight into the wind, instead of tilted upwards like that of its army prototype. The three "stabilisers" at its stern were located, and appeared to function, similarly with those of the "sausage."

The basket was mid-waist deep, and just big enough to hold comfortably two men sitting on the strips of canvas which served as seats. Supplementing our jackets, two small life-preservers of the ordinary type were lashed to the inside of the basket. When I asked about parachutes, I was told that, while it was customary to carry them, on this occasion—as they were worse than useless to a man who had not practised with them—it was best not to bother myself with one. "Stick to the basket if anything happens," some one said; "it will float for a month, even if full of water." Some one else admonished not to blow up my jacket until we had stopped rising, lest it (from the expanding air, I suppose) should in turn blow me up. Then we were off. The last thing I noticed on the deck was the ship's cat, which I had observed a few moments previously rubbing his arched back ecstatically against a sagging "stabiliser," making a wild leap to catch one of the trailing guide-ropes.

"He always does that," I heard my companion saying behind me. "Some day perhaps he will catch it, and then—if it happens at a time when there isn't an opportunity to wind in and let him down easy—I'm afraid there won't be a one of his nine lives left in the little furry pancake it will make of him when he hits the water. It's surprising how the water will flatten out a—anything striking it at the end of a thousand feet fall. Only the week before last——"

To deflect the conversation to more cheering channels, I began to exclaim about the view. And what a view it was! The old *Xerxes* was lying well down towards one end of the mighty bay, so that without turning the head one could sweep the eyes over the single greatest unit of far-reaching might in the whole world war, the Grand Fleet of the British Navy. And in no other way than in ascending in a balloon or a flying machine could one attain a vantage from which the whole of the fleet could be seen. Looking from the loftiest fore-top, from the highest hill of the islands, there was always a point in the distance beyond which there was simply an amorphous slaty blur of ships melting into the loom of the encircling land. But now those mysterious blurs were crystallising into definite lines of cleavage, and soon—save where some especially fantastic trick of camouflage made one ship look like two in collision, or played some other equally scurvy trick on the vision—I could pick out not only battleships, but cruisers, destroyers, submarines, ranged class by class and row on row. Even the method in the apparent madness with which the swarms of supply ships, colliers, oilers, trawlers, and drifters were scattered about was discernible.

Save for the visibility, which was diamond-clear in the slanting light of the low-hanging winter sun, it was just an ordinary, average Grand Fleet day. A squadron of battleships was at target practice, and—even better than their own gunnery officers—we could tally the foam-jets of the "wides" and "shorts" and the narrowing "straddles." A squadron of visiting battle-cruisers had just come to anchor and were swinging lazily round to the tide. Two of them bore names which had echoed to the ends of the world; the names of two of the others—from their distinctive lines and great size, I recognised them as twin giants I had seen still in the slips on the Clyde scarcely a year previously—the world has never heard. A lean, swift scout-cruiser, with an absence of effort almost uncanny, was cleaving its way out toward the entrance just as a line of destroyers came scurrying in after the rolling smoke-pall the following wind was driving on ahead of them. Out over the open seas to the east, across the hill-tops of the islands, dim bituminous dabs on the horizon heralded the return of a battleship squadron, the unceremonious departure of which two days previously had deprived me of the last two courses of my luncheon. In the air was another "kite"—floating indolently above a battleship at anchor—and a half-dozen circling aeroplanes and seaplanes. Countless drifters and launches shuttled in and out through the evenly lined warships.

We were now towing with the cable forming an angle of about sixty degrees with the surface of the water, and running up to us straight over the port quarter. The ship had thinned down to an astonishingly slender sliver, not unsuggestive of a speeding arrow whose feathered shaft was represented by the foaming wake.

"She's three or four points off the wind," commented my companion, "and yet—once we've steadied down—you see it doesn't make much difference in the weather we make of it. A head wind is desirable in getting up to keep from fouling the upper works amidships, but we hardly need to figure it down to the last degree as in launching a seaplane. When we're really trying to find something, of course, we have to work in any slant of wind that happens to be blowing. The worst condition is a wind from anywhere abaft the beam, blowing at a faster rate than the towing ship is moving through the water. In that case, the balloon simply drifts ahead to the end of its tether, swings around, and gives the ship a tow. If the wind is strong enough—say, forty miles an hour, with the ship doing twenty—to make her give a good steady pull on the cable, it is not so bad; but when it is touch-and-go between ship and wind the poor old 'kite' is all over the shop, and about as difficult to work in as to ride in—which is saying a good deal."

"What do you mean by work?" I asked.

"Looking out for things and reporting them to the ship over the telephone," was the reply. "Perhaps even trying to run them down and destroy them."

"Can't we play at a bit of work now?" I suggested. "Supposing we were at sea, and you saw what you thought to be the wake of the periscope of a U-boat a few miles away. What would you do?"

My companion laughed. "Well," he said, "if I had the old *Xerxes* down there on the other end of the string, I should simply report the bearing and approximate distance of the periscope over the telephone, and let her do the rest."

"And what would 'the rest' consist of?" I asked.

"Principally of turning tail and running at top speed for the nearest protected waters," was the reply, "and incidentally 'broad-casting' a wireless giving position of the U-boat and the direction it was moving in."

"But supposing it was a destroyer we had 'on the string'?" I persisted; "and that you had no other present interest in the world beyond the finding of one of these little V-shaped ripples. The *modus operandi* would vary a bit in that case, wouldn't it?"

"Radically," he admitted. "I would give the destroyer what I figured was the shortest possible course to bring her into the vicinity of the U-boat. As long as the wake of the periscope was visible, I would correct that course from time to time by ordering so many degrees to port or to starboard, as the case might be. As soon as the periscope disappeared—which it would do, of course, just as soon as the eye at the bottom of it saw the 'kite'—I would merely make a guess at the submarine's most likely course, and steer the destroyer to converge with that. Our success or failure would then hinge upon whether or not I could get my eye on the submarine where it lurked or was making off under water. In that event—provided only there was enough light left to work with—it would be long odds against that U-boat ever seeing Wilhelmshaven again. Just as you guide a horse by turning it to left or right at the tug of a rein, so, by giving the destroyer a course, now to one side, now to the other, until it was headed straight over its prey, I would guide the craft at the other end of the telephone-wire to a point from which a depth-charge could be dropped with telling effect. If the conditions were favourable, I might even be able to form a rough estimate of the distance of the U-boat beneath the surface, to help in setting the hydrostat of the charge to explode at the proper depth. If the first shot fails to do the business, we have only to double back and let off another. Nothing but the coming of night or of a storm is likely to save that U-boat once we've spotted it."

"Is it difficult to pick up a submarine under water?" I asked.

"That depends largely upon the light and the amount of sea running," was the reply. "Conditions are by no means so favourable as in the Mediterranean, but, at the same time, they are much better than in some other parts of the North Sea and the Atlantic. The condition of the surface of the water also has a lot to do with it. You can see a lot deeper when the sea is glassy smooth than when it is even slightly rippled. Waves tossed up enough to break into white-caps make it still harder to see far below the surface, while enough wind (as to-day) to throw a film of foam all over the water cuts off the view completely. On a smooth day, for instance, a drifter which lies on the bottom over there—deeper down than a U-boat is likely to go of its own free will—is fairly clearly defined from this height. To-day you couldn't find a sunk battleship there."

I remarked on the fact that, in spite of the heavy wind, our basket was riding more steadily than that of any stationary observation balloon I had ever been up in at the front. "It 'yaws' a bit," I observed, "but I have never been up in a balloon with less of that 'jig-a-jig' movement which makes it so hard to fix an object with your glasses."

"The latest 'stabilisers' have just about eliminated the troublesome 'jig-a-jig,'" replied my companion.

He turned to me with a grin. "You're in luck," he said. "Ship's heading up into the wind to let a seaplane go just as they're ready to wind us in. You'll learn, now, why they call one of these balloons a 'kite.' There they go! Hold fast!"

There was a sudden side-winding jerk, and then that perfectly good seascape—Grand Fleet, Orkneys, the north end of Scotland, and all—was hashed up into something full of zigzag lines like a Futuristic masterpiece or the latest thing in "scientific camouflaging." My friends on the deck told me, afterwards, that the basket did *not* "loop-the-loop," that it did *not* "jump through," "lie down," and "roll over" like a "clown" terrier in a circus; but how could they, who were a thousand feet away, know better than I, who was on the spot? When I put that poser to them, however, one of them replied that it was because *they* had their eyes open. The only sympathetic witness I found was one who admitted that, while the "kite" itself behaved with a good deal of dignity, the basket *did* perform some evolutions not unremotely suggestive of a canvas water-bucket swung on the end of a rope by a sailor in a hurry for his morning "souse."

COALING THE GRAND FLEET

A signal came one morning, ordering the Grand Fleet to prepare to proceed to sea, and, almost as though the sparks of the wireless that caught the winged word had themselves lighted the laid and waiting fires, wreaths and coils of smoke began crowning some scores of towering funnels which a few moments before had loomed only in gaunt silhouette against the round snow-clad hillsides which ring the Northern Base.

Presently a dust-begrimed collier shook herself free from the moorings which held her to one of the battleships, and, floundering nervously as though anxious to get out of the way as quickly as possible, nosed off into the sooty wakes of three of her untidy sisters who had been coaling the other ships of the division.

Shortly the Engineer-Commander, his immediate duties at an end for the moment, came up for a breath of fresh air, and fell into step with me on the quarter-deck.

"There you have (so far as the Navy is concerned) the Alpha and the Omega of the coal," he said, motioning with his mittened hand, first toward the retiring colliers, and then, with a sweeping gesture, to where the thickening smoke-columns were beginning to blend in a murky stratum of streaky black above the even lines of the anchored ships.

"All the energy (save only human force, and that stored in food and explosives) of the Fleet comes aboard from its colliers or oilers," he continued; "all that is left of it—after making steam to run the turbines and dynamos, and for working the condensers, cooking, and heating—goes up through the funnels or down through the clinker hoppers."

Then he told me of an incident which had occurred a day or two previously. "Some one came into the wardroom," he said, "and remarked casually that the wireless had just picked up a signal from a ship about to go ashore in the heavy storm then driving outside. 'What is she?' several officers asked with quick concern. 'Only a collier,' was the reply, and everybody, reassured, resumed the reading of their newly arrived papers. 'I was afraid it was a destroyer,' was the only comment any one made.

"That is just to show," said the Engineer-Commander, "how few in a warship (save those of us whose work is the conversion of it into energy) stop to think how vitally important coal really is to us. As a matter of fact, one can easily imagine circumstances in which the loss of a collier would be far more serious than that of a destroyer, cruiser, or even of a battleship."

It will doubtless surprise one not already informed in the matter to know that the average modern battleship lying at anchor and waiting to be ordered to sea may easily consume twenty-five tons of coal a day, which figure will be raised from 50 to 100 per cent. by one or two harbour spins at half or quarter-speed for target practice. The condensers make the greatest demand for coal in a battleship not under steam, with the running of dynamos for the numerous and constantly increasing electrical devices next in order. The galleys where the cooking and baking is done, are third on the list of consumers, with the cheery open grates—which are installed wherever practicable—accounting for the remainder.

The course of the coal from the hold of the collier to where, on the fire-bars, its potential energy is transformed into kinetic power to furnish power for a battleship is an interesting one, though I should not care to follow it quite so closely as did the ring of an officer I met not long ago. Emerging from the hold of a collier after a couple of hours spent there directing sack-filling, he missed a large signet-ring which he had been wearing when he descended into the dusty hole. Search was, of course, out of the question; but, by a lucky chance, he happened to mention his loss to one of the men who had been working in the hold. He, in turn, spoke of it in the mess-decks, which was the only reason that led the stoker, who, three days later at sea, found a shining lump of metal among the clinkers he was raking out to dump, to bring it to the officer in question. The gnarled, ash-pitted lump bore no resemblance to a ring; but a distorted, but still recognisable, section of the seal identified it beyond a doubt. It had been shovelled into a sack of coal, hoisted in the latter to the deck, dumped into a chute, finally to work out of the bottom of a bunker into the stokehold and be thrown under the boilers. A man can make the descent from the deck through an empty bunker to the stokehold without great discomfort, but would hardly survive being shut up in the former for long with the coal.

The speedy coaling of even an eight-knot tramp is almost always desirable; with a warship it may often mean the difference between success and failure. All of the principal navies of the world have given the matter much study and experiment, but down to this day no practicable contrivance has been evolved which will go far toward eliminating the variable human element in coaling. Something can be done with mechanical carriers where a ship can berth alongside high bunkers, but nothing of the kind appears to have been devised that is not too bulky to carry about in either a warship or a collier. The construction of a warship makes it impracticable to have large openings into which coal might be hoisted in bulk from a collier. The American Navy coals its battleships by hoisting that fuel to the decks with huge mechanical "grabs," but, according to such information as is available to me at this moment, this method (while effecting a saving in labour), does not approach for speed records the British have put up by man-handling the coal at every stage of its transit, except the hoisting.

Since a few minutes' time lost in the putting to sea of the million tons or so of warships which the British hold in leash against any sally in force of the German Fleet might easily be enough to spoil the chance of a decisive engagement, quick coaling has perhaps been given more attention in the Grand Fleet since the war than at any other time in the history of the British Navy. The time in which the various classes of ships can put to sea after receiving orders varies in different emergencies, and is hardly a proper topic of discussion in any detail. The coal in the bunkers of no ship is allowed to fall below a very high fixed minimum at any time, and even ships on special missions at sea always have enough in hand to allow them to reach and play a vigorous if tardy part in any conceivable kind of a general engagement that may ensue. The pursuance of this policy is responsible for the frequent and speedy coalings which are so much a feature of the regular "grind" at the Northern Base.

A ship may coal at any hour of the day or night—especially if she is just in from the sea and there appears to be a chance of her being called upon to put out again on short notice—but the usual time is the morning. Barrows and sacks are brought out, and such other preparations as practicable are made the night before. Breakfast is served at an early hour, every one—officers and men—coming down to it in their "coaling togs." The latter may be any old kind of a rig-out calculated to keep the coal-dust from penetrating to a minimum section of the hide of the wearer. A one-piece overall is a favourite garment with both men and officers, and a white summer cap-cover—worn like a cook's head-dress—serves a useful purpose in keeping the dust out of the hair. A layer of vaseline about the eyes makes it easier to remove the dust with soap and water after coaling, and a failure to take this precaution leaves one with the make-up of a moving-picture villain for two or three days. Practically all of the officers, with the exception of the paymasters and medical staff, have duties in connexion with coaling. Ordinarily, these are confined to directing various stages of the operation, but occasionally—perhaps to stimulate action when speedy work is desirable, or for the sheer exhilaration of exercise—one will take a spell with a shovel or barrow. On several ships of the Grand Fleet the *Padre* is one of the most useful "coalers."

The decks are black with waiting men as the collier comes alongside, and the instant the mooring-lines are made fast several hundred of them—each with a broad short-handled scoop—clamber over her rail and leap down into the open holds. Others toss down bundles of the sacks in which the coal is hoisted aboard. These sacks are a highly important and distinctive factor in British naval coaling, the ingenious way in which they are used being largely responsible for the remarkable speed-records which have been put up. They are made of extremely heavy jute, bound with light manilla rope, and of a size sufficient to hold two hundredweight of coal. At the mouth are two beckets or iron rings, through which the strop is rove. Each sack weighs in the neighbourhood of 16 lb., even when new; water-soaked and smeared with a paste of coal-dust, its weight may be increased by from 20 to 50 per cent. Before the war, the cost of a sack was about 11*s.* 6*d.*, but the rise in jute must have made it much greater at the present time.

The sacks are filled by scoop in the holds of the collier, and dragged together in bunches of about a dozen each. The wire cable from the hoisting-boom is run through the rings at the mouth of each sack and made fast. As the winch winds in, it tightens and takes up the slack, thus drawing the mouths of the sacks together and preventing the spilling of coal in hoisting. The instant the sacks are hoisted to the deck of the warship a man casts loose one end of the wire cable, and on the swinging back of the whip it is pulled out of the rings, and the coal left ready for the barrowmen.

The barrow employed appears to differ in no essential detail from the truck used by railway porters in handling trunks. It is perhaps a little smaller than the average of the latter, and somewhat more "squattily" built. After the "technique" of picking up and dumping one's sack is mastered, it is by no means difficult to handle, the main point being to trundle it as nearly as possible on the "balance," so that a minimum of strength is wasted in keeping the barrow from "sitting up" and "sitting down." Once these details are understood, any fairly strong man or boy should be equal to the physical exertion of coaling for two or three hours at a stretch without rest. A short, sturdily built man is at something of an advantage over a tall one, as the latter has to stoop considerably to bring his "centre of effort" behind his load.

The wheeling of the sacks, from the point where they are left in a tottering pile on the deck to the opening of the chutes down which their contents are dumped to the bunkers, is the most important stage of the operation, for the way it is carried out makes all the difference between a fast and a slow coaling. Obviously, then, it is to the organisation of this "traffic" that the greatest attention is given.

Since a battleship is primarily made for fighting, the facility with which coal may be taken aboard is necessarily a secondary consideration. Between turrets, hatches, and various other obstructions on the decks, the route by which a coal-sack is wheeled to a chute is always a devious one. Part of it usually runs across open deck, where "double-track traffic" is possible; at other points the way may be so narrow that only a single barrow can be wheeled through at a time, and even that only when carefully steered. To avoid the latter "necks," the returning "empties" must, if possible, find an alternative route, or, if this is not practicable, going and returning barrows must be "flagged" through by turn, as on a congested stretch of city street when half of it is torn up for repairs. The same sort of thing occurs where the track of the loaded barrows crosses that of the returning empties. In both instances it is customary to give "loads" the right-of-way over "empties," the latter watching their chances to push through in the frequent "gaps" in the traffic of the former. It is in the "control" of the traffic at these points, and on the quick-wittedness of the men in keeping out of each other's way and avoiding a jam, that a great part of the secret of speedy coaling lies.

But perhaps we can learn more about it by taking our barrow and falling into line. The frost-silvered metal handles strike a chill to the fingers straight through your woolly mittens; but don't worry on that score—your own animal heat will more than even-up the balance by the time you have kept your place in line for ten minutes. The last of a pile of sacks has just been trundled away, and, to the scream of the winch, another "cluster" is rising slowly out of the hold to take its place. The scoopmen are falling into their stride by this time, and from now on you can expect them to be sending up a fresh "boquet" every forty or fifty seconds. That your barrow wheels may have a fair run, a man with a scoop pushes aside the lumps of coal which have fallen out of the last sacks, and another man shovels them up and throws them into a half-filled sack hanging to the rail. There is a warning cry of "Stand clear!" and the cluster of sacks plumps down upon the deck with a heavy thud.

Even while it is still in the air two men have seized corners of the swaying mass and pushed it along so that it lands in the centre of the rather restricted working space in this particular corner of the fo'c'sle deck. At the same time, one of them frees an end of the wire cable, and, as the boom retreats, the two help to make it run smoothly out through the beckets at the mouths of the sacks. At the release of the encircling grip of the cable some of the sacks begin to topple over, but before one of them has fallen to its side (which would, of course, result in the spilling of a good part of its contents), quick-footed barrowmen have pushed their trucks under them, and they are held sufficiently upright to retain their loads. A tug or two from one of the "loading" men sets a sack straight on a barrow, and the man behind the latter—watching from the corner of an eye to keep from fouling another load—backs quickly but carefully out, executes a dexterous right-about, and trundles off on a trot along the track to the nearest chute.

After three or four barrows have been pushed impatiently past you (the wheel of one of them over the toe of your sea-boot), you suddenly realise that the dump is no place for "Alphonse and Gaston" tactics, and decide to shove in on your own. Your timid advance, however, proves too slow to head off a more pushful mate in a "sou'wester," and he gets the "lip" of his barrow under the sack you had marked for your own. You edge back politely to make an exit for him and his load, and lo!—two other "vultures" pounce in upon the pair of remaining sacks and roll away with them. You jump back towards safety at the "Dump Bosses'" shout of "Stand clear!" step in the scoop of the man who is brushing up the "crumbs," stumble against the man who has charge of the sack on the rail, and in sitting down manage to thrust your barrow between the legs of one of the men who is humouring the fresh "boquet" of coal-sacks into place. So perfect is your *camouflage* of overall, sou'-wester, and sea-boots, that none of these hasty individuals whose activities you have inadvertently interfered with recognises you as an officer and gentleman in disguise, and each of them (without arresting a single motion) curses you fluently in the picturesque persiflage of the sea.

You salve your barrow as best you can, and stand by for the withdrawal of the "strop," which is your signal for action. In your eagerness you fail to give the "lip" of your barrow that "finessive" safety-razor sweep along the deck which experience subsequently teaches you is the proper way to get under your "White Man's Burden," and give the tottering sack you are nose-diving for a vigorous dig—just the same kind of a dig that the keen-edged "lip" of the barrow you have stepped in front of gives you on your Achillean tendon. The sack totters drunkenly and sludders down upon the deck; you reach the same—less directly, but with greater impact—by caroming off the barrow which has slashed your heel.

A spilled sack—in clogging the nicely adjusted coaling machine—always has the germ of a jam lurking in it, and only the two or three stout fellows who buck their laden barrows straight through the mess you have made—by clearing the last of the sacks away a hair's breadth before the next "boquet" descends upon them—avert disaster now. Luckily, they are able to swear and work at the same time, and, by plying their hands no less vigorously than their tongues, save the situation.

The man who throws the "crumbs" into the sack on the rail is less busy than the other dump hands, and he it is who finds leisure to insinuate that you ought to go to some place where they have no coaling to do. You have no time to consider whether he means—the place you would mean if you were in his place; for your honour is at stake now, and, scowling with grim, coldly calculative determination, you stand for the third trial. Neither too coy nor yet too impulsive this time, but by the exercise of such common sense as is still at your command, you press quietly but firmly toward the cluster of sacks and—by lifting your barrow bodily and jerking it sidewise for a few inches—manage to align it fairly evenly in front of a bulging bag of coal dust. It appears to require about as much effort on the part of one of the "load" hands to wriggle it aboard as it does on your part to tip back your barrow to something like a balance. But the fact remains that you *do* have it stowed, and are ready to get under weigh.

It is the "coldly calculative, set-jaw" spirit which carries you through the next stage with fair success. It is no easy task to do your "right-about" on the slithery deck, but now that you are a "load" instead of an "empty" a tendency to help you on your way is at once in evidence. A couple of "empties" are edged back an inch or two to give you clearance, and a "load" accelerates to avoid giving you a "sideswipe." Where the deck slopes up under the elevated midship guns the petty officer who stands there to wave the traffic down the proper passage gives your sack a friendly kick to keep your barrow from losing weigh and checking the pushers crowding close on your heels.

You debouch to open deck on the port side and are about to push on in the wake of the man just ahead, when the corner of your eye catches the motion of the left-hand of the "traffic officer," and—with the going easy on the down slope—you execute a neat eight-point alteration of course and bring up smartly in front of an open "man-hole" just in time to replace a man who has dumped his sack and ducked out of your way. Unluckily, you have had no chance to study the "technique" of this operation, and it is not surprising that you run too close and dump your sack so that it falls with its mouth a foot beyond the hole and disgorges a part of its contents on the deck. As a consequence, the two men working here have to drag the sack back before emptying it, where (if you had dumped it properly) they would only have had to lift it by its corners and allow the coal to run out down the chute. Of course, they tell you what they think of you, and while you are answering that you are sorry for your mistake and will know how to avoid it next time, a sharp dig from an only half-checked barrow "lip" on your already wounded "Achilles tendon" helps to drive home the rule that—while there is no ban on talking, swearing and singing to your heart's content—the action of the tongue should not be allowed to paralyse the action of the feet.

The man ahead of you has disappeared at a trot, and in your eagerness to overtake him you lift the handles of your barrow too high, with the consequence that the first lump of coal that gets under the wheels brings it up standing, and you "telescope" against it. The lesson this drives home to you, together with the one that sinks in following the jam you create by your slowness in plunging through the procession of "loads" which must be passed in getting back to the dump, just about rounds out the basic essentials of your barrow-pushing education. You have learned how to keep out of the way; the rest is largely a matter of handling your barrow in a fashion to make the work easier, not only for yourself, but for the others whose operations "dovetail" with yours.

The work in the holds of the collier and the bunkers of the battleship, while perhaps a shade less strenuous physically than barrow-pushing, is a deal more dusty and unpleasant. Four holds are worked in the average collier, and in each of these are about thirty men. These work in six groups, each of which fills and stacks one "cluster" of sacks. The men alternate in holding sacks and shovelling. Special instructions are given that the sacks shall be completely filled, and that no pieces of coal too large to go down the chutes to the bunkers should be put in them. A maul is kept handy in each hold for smashing such lumps. A minimum of a dozen sacks are hoisted at one time, and occasionally this number is increased by two or three.

The coal dust is the unpleasant feature of working in the holds of the colliers, but even there it is nothing to the bunkers, where one actually feels it grinding between his teeth from the moment he enters. The coal falls in a steady stream from the chutes, the dust flying from it like the spray from a waterfall. There is no electric wiring, and the lights are open flares, good ventilation making the danger of an explosion from coal "damp" negligible. The men who work here shovelling the coal away from the chutes and passing it on toward the lower bunkers—would make the average chimney-sweep look like a white-winged angel. There is no way to avoid inhaling the settling dust with every breath, and I could well believe a red-eyed imp o' darkness (whom I found blinking like a bat in the sunshine after the collier had cast off) when he told me that he would be tasting the "bloomin' stuff for the next week."

The more one sees of coaling the more he marvels at the extent to which the human element enters into its success. A crew that is not both quick of foot and quick of wit will never have more than a mediocre coaling record. If a man has not both, when he is not getting in the way of his mates, he will be losing a few seconds here, and a few seconds there, until these run into minutes in the course of two or three hours. Multiplied by five or six hundred—the number of the men at work—it may well make the difference in a coaling rate of many score of tons per hour.

A keen interest and pride in the work is also a *sine qua non* of fast coaling. No ship in which there is not the best of feeling between the men and officers will ever maintain a high coaling average. Under the stimulus of imminent action, or when preparing to weigh anchor for some favourite port, things will move quickly, but the rate will not be maintained when the regular grind resumes. Indeed, slow coaling is, perhaps, the commonest form of "silent protest" on the part of a dissatisfied crew, and a ship which maintains a steadily depressed "curve of coaling" is generally credited with being due for a general shake-up of personnel.

THE STOKERS

Except for the actual lift she receives from a wave, a battleship rolling in a beam sea moves a good deal like an inverted pendulum, so that one feels a minimum of motion when he is down against the skin of a lower hold and the maximum in the foretop. The transition had been a sudden one for me that morning, for the Gunnery Lieutenant, who had been initiating me into the secrets of "Director Firing" in the foretop, brought me back to the main deck and turned me over to the Senior Engineer, who had volunteered to show me what "rough weather" stoking was like.

The big ship was wallowing with that ever-disconcerting "hang" at the end of a roll, such a pause as one never experiences in an ocean liner which (with no heavy guns and only light upper works) needs no great amount of time to make up its mind as to whether or not it is worth while going to the trouble of getting back on an even keel. As we put one reeling steel ladder after another above us in our descent, the roll decreased as the tumult of crashing waves was stilled to muffled jolts, and, with a flight or two still to go, we were steady enough on our feet to have both hands free to lift the heavy air-tight "flap" of the boiler-room.

As I ducked under the "flap" the chill, damp, clammily clinging air of the decks above was assailed by a sharp blast which, however hot and dry, was still (at least in comparison with the heavy atmosphere of the higher 'tween decks spaces) fresh and invigorating. Although far from an earthly paradise in a ship on an equatorial run, the stokehold of a battleship that is battened down against heavy winter weather is in some respects the most comfortable spot aboard her.

Certainly the half-dozen brawny fellows who sat or lounged against the steel bulkhead of the half of the boiler-room into which we had descended did not look to be having anything like so bad a time of it as an equal number of oilskinned seamen I had seen but a few minutes before bracing themselves against the seas sweeping the icy forecastle deck as they tried to repair a smashed ventilator. Grimy they were, to be sure, but otherwise there was little about them to suggest the sweating, stripped-to-the-waist, in-to-the-last-gasp stoker of romance and popular fancy.

To one who has pictured the stoker as a gaunt-eyed demon steadily shovelling coal under a boiler for four hours, the first glimpse of a stokehold of a warship that is in no great hurry to get somewhere will come as a good deal of a surprise. The place is neither especially dirty nor especially hot. Neither the letting the coal slide down by its own weight from the encompassing bunkers nor the cracking up of the occasional lumps which are too large for even combustion raises as much dust as the dumping of a single sack upon one of the upper decks.

The footing on the grilled steel plates of the deck is firm and sure, and, as I have said, there is less motion in the stokehold than in any other part of the ship. It might conceivably happen in destroyers, but the stories of men half-roasted from being thrown against the furnace doors in storms do not originate on battleships.

But let us see how these comfortable, easy-moving chaps manage to handle the fuel sufficient to send twenty-five or thirty thousand tons of steel hurtling through the seas with so little apparent haste or effort. The running back of a sliding steel door brings a stream of coal running out of one of the bunkers, coal which, dumped from sacks into the entrance of a chute on one of the upper decks, has worked its way downward by gravity as that beneath it has been fed to the furnaces. This stream is caught in a "skip" of steel, shaped like the half of a cylinder and capable of holding something like a couple of hundredweight. Sliding fairly easily over the grilled deck—pushed by one man and pulled by another—the "skip" loads are dumped evenly along in front of the twelve doors which open—four to each—to the three furnaces under the boilers occupying this half of the stokehold. Now we come to the actual stoking.

A bell suddenly clangs, echoing sharply from the steel walls, and instantly two of the lounging figures quicken to the alert. One scoops up a shovelful of coal and the other steps forward and rests a hand on the lever running to one of the furnace doors. A second or two later, as a number shows on a dial at the side, the latter pushes the lever sharply, and the door is pressed upwards, revealing a glowing bed of fire running back out of sight under the boiler. The shovel is already swinging forward as the door rises, and, missing that steel plate by a fraction of an inch, its contents are discharged—with a quick "wristy" motion which scatters the coal evenly over the fire—into the furnace.

As the shovel is drawn back the lever is released, permitting the door to fall shut of its own weight. With all possible speed another scoop is filled with coal and the operation repeated once or twice more according to the speed which it is desired to maintain. Then the two men relax and stand at ease until another clanging of the bell heralds the number of the next furnace to be fired. Then the door is lifted and the coal thrown in as before, the operation going on until each of the twelve has received its two, three, or four shovels, when—always subject to the indicator on the wall—it begins over again.

If a lump of coal is larger than a man's fist it is cracked up before being thrown into the furnace. As the stoker swings his filled shovel toward the opening door his trained eye is looking for two things—a pronounced hollow in the bed of coals, or a spot in which the duller glow tells him the combustion is considerably advanced. If neither is visible he gives his shovel a very sharp side flirt and spreads its contents just as widely and evenly as he possibly can. If he observes a hollow he endeavours to even it up with fresh coal. A burnt-out spot also receives fresh fuel, and if there is evidence of the formation of a crust of "clinker," this may be marked for a subsequent cracking up with the "slice," a long steel bar which serves the purpose of a poker. Every effort is bent toward maintaining a smooth, evenly burning bed of coals under all of the boiler.

Automatic regulation of stoking is no new thing in warships, and was even in use on the latest of the Atlantic liners running before the war. The machine most commonly in use by the British is the "Kilroy," and its object is to raise a given amount of steam with a minimum of coal and physical effort.

Thoroughly to understand its workings one should go first to the engine-room, from where it is regulated. The order for a certain speed is sent from the bridge to the engine-room, and the engineer sets his "Kilroy" so that the stoking shall proceed at a rate calculated to produce the necessary steam. The dial of the machine is numbered from "3" to "12," and the number he turns the indicator to—say "7"—rings up the numbers of the furnace doors in the boiler-room at a rate which will ensure that each shall be stoked every seven minutes.

The number of shovelfuls of coal to be thrown in at each stoking is determined by consulting first the telegraph from the bridge (which registers in both the engine-room and stokehold) and a table which each stoker knows by heart. The dial of the telegraph is marked as follows: "Keep Steam," "Stop," "Slow," "Half Speed," "Full Speed," "More Steam." The table referred to gives the number of shovels to be thrown on at each stoking to fulfil the direction on the telegraph. Thus "Slow" calls for from two to three shovels of coal, "Full" four to six, and "More Steam" from six to eight.

This plan gives perhaps the most perfect control of stoking possible without mechanical handling of the coal, and that is hardly practicable on shipboard. Practically all modern coal-burning ships carry a small supply of oil fuel, which is, however, generally used very sparingly and kept for raising steam pressure quickly in great emergency.

It was while I was being initiated into the technique of stoking by shovelling coal under the boilers at the rate indicated to keep the steam at "Half" that a change of course brought the swinging seas dead abeam and set the ship rolling even more drunkenly than before. After failing to hit the "dark spots" and "hollows" two or three times as I staggered to the roll, and once even missing the furnace door itself, one of the stokers, taking compassion, relieved me of the scoop and put the trouble right with half a dozen quickly tossed shovelfuls.

I was frankly glad to work over to where I could take a "half Nelson" round a bar by the starboard bunker, for the way the open mouth of the furnace was suddenly jumping up at me in the lurches was something more than disconcerting, especially after one of my fellow stokers had told me that his scarred forearm was the result of having once been pitched forward against a red-hot door of the furnace under a destroyer's boiler.

It was easy to see that stoking the furnaces of a ship with a 25 to 30 degree roll is no job for a novice. Keeping one's balance without holding on to something was difficult enough all of the time, and there were intervals when it was a sheer impossibility. Yet the inexorable gong rang out its warnings just the same, and when the number of the door to be stoked slipped into place on the dial, the particular stretch of glowing coals commanded by that aperture had to be fed willy-nilly.

With the coal "skip" doing a dervish dance from one end to the other of the narrow space, and with even lumps of the coal itself indulging in punitive expeditions on their own account, the waiting stoker needed all the quick-wittedness and shifty-footedness of a bull-fighter combined with the nicety of balance of a tight-rope walker to carry on at all. Yet carry on he did, and with only less clocklike a regularity than the imperturbable "Kilroy" itself.

A heavy slam-banging from the opposite end of the boiler-room indicated that things were not going quite so smoothly there, and edging cautiously along I was presently able to get some hint of the cause from the words of a volubly cursing stoker who limped out to tell me that the "blinkin' skip 'as took charge." Rubbing a bruised shin and glowering balefully from a blackened eye which appeared to have bumped against a boiler, he explained, in language more forceful than elegant, that some unpractical theorist had encouraged them to experiment with wheels on the side of the skip with the idea of making it easier to push about over the coal-cluttered deck. This had turned out a very satisfactory "safe-in-harbour" expedient, but the increased mobility which had been so useful in fair weather had proved its undoing in foul.

In the picturesque language of the sea, it had "taken charge," and so effectually that one swift, straight rush to starboard, followed by a "googly" progress back to port, put every man who, either by chance or intent, barred its way more or less *hors de combat*. When I peeped gingerly round a corner the sight I saw was vividly suggestive of those good old days of mass play American football when a burly half-back was bucking the line of his demoralised opponents.

The heavy three-quarters-full skip had slammed down against the port bunkers when the ship rolled to that side, and in the second or two she hung there before swinging back again half a dozen men had thrown themselves upon it in an effort to "clip its wings" by removing the wheels. Either the time was too short, or else they had got in each other's way.

At any rate, the wheels were still in position to go round when the battleship, sliding down the reverse of the big wave that had thrown her over, tilted her decks back the other way. Straight down the one-in-three incline from the port to the starboard bunkers lolloped the Juggernaut, dashing the protesting anatomies of the stokers to left and right as it went. Spitting blood and oaths indiscriminately, one man clung to it all the way, however, and he it was who, taking advantage of the tilt, finally rendered it harmless by pushing it over on its side, where it was left wriggling impotently like an overturned turtle.

Meanwhile the "Kilroy" had been ringing up its numbers in vain, and it took several minutes of fast shovelling by all hands to bring the fires up to where they would have been had the interruption not occurred.

It was about this time that the bridge called on the engine-room for an increase of speed, and it was that, with a change of course, that sent the mounting seas crashing over the starboard bow, which brought my visit to the stokeholds to a sudden and unceremonious end. There came a shivering crash, followed by a momentary halt like that which throws one against his neighbour in a jerkily-braked tramcar.

The great ship staggered groggily for a second or two as a weight of solid water equal to her own was launched against her. Then the relentless urge of her spinning screws drove her forward, with the dish of her rigid hull skimming a few thousand tons off the top of the uprearing wave that had assailed her. The most of the mighty cataclysm surged to lee and back into the sea again, but wherever there was an opening—by gun-port, by ventilator, by unbattened hatch—it poured below in thunderous torrents. Deck by deck, where we had descended so laboriously by tilting ladders, we heard it bounding lower and lower, and then (just how and by where I never exactly understood) the flood was all about us.

"If we ship two or three more like that it'll be getting to the fires," shouted the warrant officer who had taken me over from the Senior Engineer; "we'll only be in the way here; we'd best get up while we can. I've stood all the watches I care to in flooded stokeholds in the years I was a stoker myself."

Over steel plates that were rocking with the wash of the water that had penetrated beneath them, he led me to a little electric lift into which the two of us were just able to crowd and slide the door. "Never thought much of this thing," he said as the car began to ascend after two or three propitiatory prods at the button; "there's too much chance of getting stalled halfway and spending the night like a tinned herring. But even that would be better than getting caught by another waterfall on one of the ladders. Besides, she seems to be going all right anyway."

Half a minute later the little lift came to a creaking standstill, and we squeezed out to a ladder which led up to the main deck. The wash swirled to our knees in an angle of the mess-deck, but the warrant officers' mess, to which I was conducted by my guide, was warm and dry. Toasting bread for our tea in the genial glow of the electric heater, he told me yarns of the days when he himself had (to use his own picturesque expression) "stood at the small end of a shovel" before the furnace doors.

He had once been scalded with escaping steam in the hold of an old cruiser off the coast of South America, once imprisoned in the stokehold of a destroyer for forty-eight hours in a gale in the sub-Arctic, and once he had been "mentioned" for putting out a fire started by a German shell in some nondescript craft in which he found himself at the time the British Navy was trying to protect the retreat along the Flemish coast. The latter sounded like a "story," and I threw a "lead" or two to draw it out. This was about all I got.

"The old *Flighty* got in too close," he said, turning the slice on his toasting fork, "and the Huns opened up on us with bigger stuff than we reckoned they had there. There was a big crash, just like when a big lump of sea hits you, only worse, and all the stokers and me (I was a petty officer then) was knocked flat. We were under forced draught, and the fires needing all the coal we could pitch on to them. No one was much hurt, and I got them to shovelling again as soon as I could. Then I took a squint up the ventilator down which most of the shock seemed to come.

"There was a bit of a fire getting under way up there, and so I pitched up two or three buckets of water and put it out. Didn't notice till afterwards that a small fragment of shell had come down and hit me in the forehead— right here" (touching a jagged cut just under the hair).

"Captain seemed rather pleased about it, as the men on fire station in that part of the ship had been knocked out, and he appeared to think I had kept the blaze from getting a big headway.

"'Nother funny thing"—and he went on to tell of a stoker of a trawler who, after having his face slightly scalded by steam, had lain down and gone to sleep with his head pillowed among some of the steward's recent purchases, and of how the cook, foraging in the twilight and starting to pick up what he thought was a boiled lobster, had nearly pulled off one of the unlucky chap's burned ears!

I sought the fo'c'sle deck for a breath of fresh air after that, and pushed my head out of the after superstructure just as a hulking cinder came winging aft before the snoring north-east gale. It was quite possible (I said to myself as I ducked inside and pulled down my eyelid in an endeavour to deposit the unwelcome fragment on my cheek) that this very cinder was one which I myself had dumped down one of the bunker chutes during our last coaling.

At any rate, I knew that, save for that last leg skywards by way of the furnaces, I had followed the path of the coal from the collier to the funnel-top, and even a bit further. I had, therefore, no legitimate cause for resentment over the fact that it had taken to following me.

III. AMERICA ARRIVES

THE UNITED STATES NAVY

In writing some months ago on the coming of the American Army to France, I quoted the naïve words used by a French Staff Officer to describe the impression the new arrivals had made upon him. After speaking of the keenness of the American officers to learn from those who had had the experience, he concluded: "We like them very much. In fact, they have been quite a surprise. They have not displayed the least tendency to show us how to run the war. Indeed, *they are not the least American!*"

I do not know that I have heard a British naval officer use *precisely* the same words in voicing his relief that his American "opposite number," whom he is now beginning to meet with increasing frequency and intimacy, has not fulfilled expectations in insisting on showing the British Navy how to win the war; but that precise sentiment I heard implied many times, though, I am happy to record, less and less frequently as the favourable impression formed by those who have had opportunity of meeting the first officers from across the Atlantic, has had time to "percolate." Save on the score of technical training and uniform, there is very little to differentiate the American naval officer from his brother in the Army who has furnished so agreeable a surprise to his Allies in France, and there need be no fear (whatever may have been expected from those who have not had the opportunity of meeting him before) that the former will not "keep station" at sea in the same quiet unostentatious way that the latter has "fallen into step" on land.

So far, since American naval activities in the war zone have been largely limited to the operations of their fleet of destroyers off the Irish coast, the two navies have had far less opportunity to get acquainted than have the British and American armies. The liaison established at Queenstown, however, may be taken as a microcosm of the co-operation that will be established on a larger scale should the exigencies of the situation demand it. As thoroughly characteristic of the spirit in which the Americans are taking up their work in these waters, I may quote the words of an officer of one of their destroyers with whom I talked recently.

"Green as we came to the job," he said, "in comparison to their three years of hard experience of the British, our taking over here was almost like a lot of boy scouts replacing a regiment of seasoned veterans in the trenches. We were all for the job, however, and somehow we began to get results right from the get-away. Let me tell you, though, that if we had had to find out all the wrinkles of the game ourselves—if they had not given us the benefit of all they had been paying in ships and men for three years to learn—it would have been a far slower business for us, and a far more costly one as well. I take off my hat to the British destroyers and trawlers, and to the men who man them. I have not had a chance yet to see anything of the rest of their Navy, but if the officers and men are of the same stamp as those we have worked with here, when our capital ships come over it will be just like joining up with another American fleet."

These sentiments seem to me thoroughly typical of the spirit with which the American Navy is taking up its task in European waters, and such also was the opinion of a distinguished British Naval officer to whom I quoted them not long ago.

"I have known American Naval Officers a good many years," he said, "principally on the China and West India stations, so that, personally, I had none of the doubts about our ability to co-operate with them that may have been harboured by some of my friends who had been less fortunate than myself on that score. The fact that the average untravelled Briton has had to judge the American wholly by such specimens as seemed to him the most characteristic among those coming to this side of the water—that is, by the Cook's tourist and the money-slinging millionaire, neither of whom is in the least representative—has been responsible for our getting, as a nation, a distorted picture of you, as a nation. It was that which gave the more conservative element in both our Army and Navy some doubts as to how we might settle down to pull in double harness.

"One of the best things about the American Naval Officer—and one that stands him in good stead at the present time—is his open-mindedness. He may have come over here firmly believing that some gun, some explosive, some system of loading or fire-control, or any of a number of other things he has perfected to the best of his experience, is better than anything else of the kind that Britain or any other nation has got. But that does not blind him in the least to the good points of the latter, and no false sentiment, pride, or conservatism will prevent the incontinent scrapping of his own long-laboured-over invention to make way for what his open mind and sterling common sense tell him is better. It is this which makes it comparatively easy for the American to do a thing which is above almost all others difficult for the Briton—to profit and take advantage of another's experience.

"An American destroyer—and the same will be true of any other ships of whatever class that may be sent over—takes its place as a unit of one of our fleets or squadrons just as easily and naturally as if a new British ship, manned by British sailors, had been commissioned, and that will go on just as long as it is necessary or advisable to increase your naval strength in European waters. Indeed, the effective smoothness of the system under which the American ships work with ours makes one feel that—quite without realising it—we have taken the first step in the formation of what has so long been talked of as a Utopian dream—an 'International Police Force.' It is hardly the time to talk of such a consummation at this stage of things; but if it ever does eventuate, you make take it that an Anglo-Saxon naval force will be its foundation."

Because it has been impossible to tell the public really anything about American naval co-operation with the British, the historic significance of that event has been almost overlooked. As a matter of fact, however, it marks the first occasion in which the ships of one Allied nation have been practically incorporated (so far as the direction of operations are concerned) in the navy of another. Allied fleets have carried out operations together—as the French and the British at the Dardanelles, or the British and the Italians in the Adriatic—but never has the co-operation been so intimate—and, it may be added, so successful—as in the present instance.

That the British and American naval officer would "hit it off" well personally from the outset no one with any acquaintance with both of them could ever have had any doubt. As a matter of fact, indeed, there is less difference between them than between the average American and Englishman, and even that is a good deal less than most people imagine. In the first place, they come from very nearly the same classes socially (I am speaking now of the regular "R.N." and "U.S.N."), in their respective countries, and there is very little indeed to differentiate the English lad of thirteen or fourteen and the American lad of a year or two older, the one beginning his naval training at Osborne and the other at Annapolis. Differing in details though they are, the training of these two naval schools is far less divergent than that of English and American public schools and universities. That is to say, the naval schools of the two countries are aiming at precisely the same thing—the turning out of an officer who knows his business—whereas public schools and universities are working in a number of different directions.

The system of appointing the American naval cadet ensures that each year's class is selected as nearly as may be from all parts of the country. Each member of the Congress is required to make one appointment to both the naval and military academies, and, in addition to these, there are ten or more appointments at large made from Washington. In this way each State is represented in the Naval Academy according to its population. Thus New York, with, say, forty members in the House of Representatives and two in the Senate, would have forty-two nominees, while Nevada, with three members in the House and two in the Senate, would have five. A Member of Congress has his choice of making the appointment open to a competitive examination or giving it direct to any boy fulfilling the requisite requirements. Even in the latter case, however, the prospective nominee must pass very stiff examinations calculated to establish his mental, moral, and physical fitness, and it is practically impossible for him to be pushed in simply because he has friends in high places. It is, I believe, becoming more and more the custom to resort to competitive examination, so that the boy named by each member is usually the brightest of a score or more striving for that honour from his Congressional district, which contains, roughly, a population of from two to three hundred thousand.

As nearly as the comparison can be made, the four-years' course at the Annapolis Naval Academy covers about the same ground that the British cadet covers in his two years at Osborne, the same period (since the war somewhat reduced) at Dartmouth, and his first year as a midshipman. Since the average age of entrance to Osborne is about thirteen and a half, and to Annapolis about sixteen, it is difficult to compare the entrance requirements or the courses. As the British cadet has about two and a half years the start of the American in the matter of age, it follows that the latter—to reach an equality of training, if not of rank, at twenty—must cover in four years the same ground which the former does in six and a half. This, I should say, he comes pretty near to accomplishing.

The fact that the American Navy was less than half of the size of the British, while the population from which officers could be drawn was more than twice that of the British Isles, made it possible for Annapolis to insist on a mental and physical standard in its entrants calculated to make them equal to the very stiff years of work ahead of them. The system of naming as "alternative" the boy who passed "No. 2" in the competitive entrance examination also made it possible to weed out and replace in the first year any cadet who began to lag behind his class.

Not only was the "book" and class-room work at Annapolis a good deal stiffer than in the corresponding years at Osborne and Dartmouth, but the year was a longer one in point of work. At Osborne the cadet spent three terms of three months each, with the other three months of the year divided into his Easter, Summer, and Christmas holidays. At Annapolis there was something like nine months of work at the academy proper, with the summer months spent in cruising on a training ship.

At the end of four years—or at about the age of twenty—the American cadet, on passing the examinations, received the rank of ensign—corresponding to the British sub-lieutenant—and began his sea career as an officer. The British midshipman usually managed to qualify for his first stripe at a somewhat earlier age than his American cousin, and this start tended to increase rather than decrease as he climbed the ladder of promotion. Speaking very roughly the British lieutenant appears to average two or three years younger than his American "opposite," the lieutenant-commander three or four, the commander three to five, and the captain five to seven.

Of the training of the cadets in the British and American naval institutions, only the briefest comparison is possible here. On the physical side there is very little difference, both giving the greatest encouragement to outdoor exercise and bodily development. Each pays equal attention to aquatics—rowing, swimming, and sailing—and American football gives the Annapolis cadet the same vigorous, manly training as "rugger" does those of Osborne and Dartmouth. Baseball and cricket are more or less in the same class.

On the technical side there was also a good deal of similarity in the training, though it seems probable that the "specialisation," which is the principal differentiation between the British and American Naval Officer (who is given an "all-round" preparation), is being given more and more attention in the British schools as the necessity of turning out officers rapidly has increased during the war. The fact that it is the British rather than the American officer who is trained as a "specialist" presents a curious anomaly, for, generally speaking, the United States is, of all the nations in the world, the one where specialisation is carried to the greatest length. Yet the fact remains that it has always been the American practice not only to train the naval cadet so that he is competent ultimately to perform the duties of any officer on any ship of the Navy, but actually to require him to serve several years in each of such various capacities as engineer, navigator, gunnery, or torpedo officer.

This system gives the officer who has been "through the mill" an incomparable experience by the time he attains his captaincy, but the number of good men (who might have made most excellent specialists) who "fell by the wayside" because they were not able to stand the pace for qualifying for so great a range of duties makes one doubt if it is practicable for any nation situated otherwise than was the United States up to its entry into the present war—that is, with a huge population and a modest navy. With the development of the modern man-of-war, the increasing mastery of technical detail which such duties of those of torpedo or gunnery officer entail would seem to make it inevitable that such officers should not be required to divert their attention or energies to anything else. This fact we may confidently expect to see reflected both in the training of the cadet at Annapolis and in American naval practice before very long—perhaps even during the war.

The fact that—as was only natural—the United States Navy, when it was formed during the Revolutionary War, was modelled on the only other Navy of which the colonials had experience—the British—is responsible for many similarities in the forms and practices of the respective services to-day. The gold sleeve or shoulder stripes indicating the rank of officers are practically identical, save only that the Americans replace the British executive "curl" with a star. The American Marine even retains the silver half-globe which is so characteristic a feature of the badge of the Royal Marine of the British Navy. In manning guns, and even whole turrets, with Royal Marines, it would appear that the British Navy has progressed rather further than has the American from the time when this "anachronistic amphibian," as some one has called him, was carried principally to swarm over the rail with a cutlass when the old ships of the line closed in a death grapple. In general multifarity of duties, however, there is little to choose between this always useful "soldier-and-sailor-too" of either service.

The comparatively short term of service in the American Navy was responsible for the fact that the Yankee man-o'-war's-man was a good deal less of a "jolly Jack Tar" in appearance than his British cousin, a difference which has been accentuated since America entered the war by the necessity of an even further "dilution" of landsmen. The practice of allowing the American sailor to wear a sweater and toboggan cap, except on "dress" occasions, has also tended to make him smack less of the sea than the flowing-collared sailor-man who will be performing similar duties on a British ship. Since the fighting of the modern warship is about 90 per cent. "mechanical" and 10 per cent. "nautical," however, the lack of the "Yo-heave-ho" touch in the Yankee sailor-man is by no means in his disfavour. On the contrary, indeed, the very fact that he has only just come to sea may indicate that he has spent all the more time in mastering the intricacies of machinery and electricity and the other things which enter so much into the efficiency of the present-day fighting-ship.

To quote my American naval friend again, both navies have many things that are different—in ships, guns, engines, executive system, victualling—and each may feel a natural pride in its own things. There is undoubtedly much in each navy the other can profit by, but the United States Navy is bearing in mind that everything new the British Navy has to offer it has been tried and proved by long and hard experience, while all the new things it is able to offer the British Navy have only been put to peace-time tests. But now that American ships are having practical experience, that is being altered rapidly.

"GETTING TOGETHER"

I. How the Officers of the British and American Ships that are working together in European Waters are making each other's Acquaintance

Perhaps the most gratifying tribute I have heard paid to the American Battle Squadron which has been for many months incorporated in and working with the Grand Fleet was an unconscious one.

"How are the Americans getting on?" I asked an officer of the Commander-in-Chief's staff a few days ago.

"The Americans?" he repeated. "Oh, you mean the 'Xth B. S.' They have merged so completely into the Grand Fleet that we long ago ceased to think of them as anything but a part of ourselves. Indeed, that's just what they have become—a part of ourselves. They're doing their part. I couldn't say more for them."

The world was a good deal impressed when, just after the German offensive started last March, President Wilson, acting on General Pershing's suggestion, agreed to the brigading of the American troops in France with the British and French armies until such time as they were in sufficient strength to form an army of their own. It was a wise action from the military point of view alone, but doubly so in giving our allies so unmistakable example of the spirit in which America was entering the common fight.

It is characteristic of the essential difference between land and sea operations that the announcement of a similar sacrifice of national pride in the furtherance of Allied unity—this time on the part of the American Navy, and antedating the other by several months—should have to be withheld from the public until the significance of it was largely overshadowed by the more dramatic conditions under which the decision to brigade the American troops with the Allied armies was taken. Yet it is a fact that, until the arrival of the American battleships, white with brine of the Atlantic across which they had ploughed their way, last winter, never before in history had the warships of one nation endeavoured to co-operate with those of another save as a separate fleet. Never, indeed, up to that time, had such a consummation been deemed practicable.

But the American Navy Department and—especially—the distinguished Admiral appointed to the command of the first squadron to be sent to European waters, realising that nothing but national pride, and certain service practices which they felt sure Yankee adaptability would be equal to modifying, were the only obstacles to an arrangement which could not but add incalculably to the weight they were throwing into the balance, decided—quite on their own initiative and without any pressure whatever from the British—that all American battleships should be incorporated into the Grand Fleet instead of operating as a distinct American force. From that time on, to all intents and purposes, it was as though so many new British units—fresh from the yards of the Tyne or the Clyde—had been added to the Grand Fleet. The American ships still flew the Stars and Stripes, and there were no changes in pay, uniform, discipline, nor in such technical practices as effected the efficiency of the ship as a fighting unit. But in every particular involving relations with the Grand Fleet as a whole, British practice was and is the rule. Everything that any British ship or squadron does devolves likewise upon every American ship and squadron, this extending from such things as providing work-parties for road-making or other jobs on the beach, to sallying forth on one of the great concerted sweeps through the North Sea in which the bulk of the floating might of the whole world is on the move.

One American battleship which, crossing the Atlantic alone and arriving at Base only a few hours before the Grand Fleet was ordered to sea on what at the moment looked like the hottest kind of a Hun scent, made a great hit with the sport-loving British by replenishing her bunkers in a wildly-rushed coaling, and raising steam in time to get under weigh, and swing into line with her sisters who had been grooming themselves for just such an event for many weeks. The next morning I was standing on the bridge of a British super-dreadnought with an historic name, when the Admiral read out a signal from the Fleet Flagship, which made it appear likely that an action with the German High Sea Fleet was but a matter of a few hours. Walking out to the end of the bridge, he turned his glasses back to where, steaming hard in line ahead, the American ships were coming up in perfect station on our starboard quarter. Running his glasses back along the line, he rested his glance for a moment on the last ship.

"There's the good old *Texas*," he said, with an affectionate smile, "not an inch out of station, and steaming with the best of 'em. You'd never think to see her that she was bucking the swells of the Atlantic at this time yesterday morning. My word, what a stroke of luck for her if she *does* happen to stumble, in her first twenty-four hours with the Grand Fleet, into what the rest of us have been waiting four years for!"

It turned out to be the same old disappointment after all, this time as so many others, but the plucky bid the *Texas* made for a chance of participating in "Der Tag" pleased the British mightily, and won her at the outset a high place in their esteem.

That the newcomers would have much to learn from the three- and four-year veterans of the Grand Fleet was only to be expected, and right eagerly they set themselves out to master the things that can only be taught by experience. But the exchange of ideas was not entirely one-sided. One day I heard the Gunnery Lieutenant of my ship speaking with great enthusiasm of the American telephone system, and of the astonishing speed with which the "Yanks" loaded their turret guns. The Commander came back from U.S.S. *New York* loud in the praise of the quality of the American paints, which he claimed gave a surface much more easily kept clean than the similar grades provided in the British ships. The swift, smart American launches always evoked favourable comment, and even the strange-looking "bird-cage" masts won occasional converts. Perhaps the most interesting thing of all is the large and increasing number of British officers that one hears speaking sympathetically, and even approvingly, of the total abstinence in force in the American ships. The fact that the officers of the latter are practically unanimous in declaring that they would never favour going back to the old regime has made a good deal of an impression on the British, and more and more frequently I hear the older Royal Naval officers saying that they wished they had the same anti-liquor rules in force in their own ships.

In these and a score of other similar things one has evidence every day that, while the British Fleet is a constant inspiration to the Americans, the coming of the latter has not been without its "tonic" effects on the former.

Social entertainment between ship and ship is one of the features of British naval life that has been most conspicuous by its absence since the war began, and perhaps the highest compliment that could be paid the Americans was that the Grand Fleet did not consider it necessary to make any exception to the general practice in their case. Senior and Junior officers of ships that chanced to be moored conveniently near each other lunched and dined back and forth, but no more or no less than if the newcomers had been English rather than American. There was no drinking of high-sounding toasts, and the nearest thing to formality in this respect I recall was the proposing the health of "The President," following that of "The King," with the port. For the rest, when one of our Latin allies could not possibly resist clinking glasses to "America," "The Entente," "Victory," and no end of similar toasts, the Briton contented himself with an unobtrusive "Cheerio" or "Chin-chin."

But what these little unpremeditated "inter-wardroom" affairs lacked in formality they made up in geniality. One of the most memorable "evenings" I ever spent was that following a dinner in a certain famous light cruiser of the Australian Navy, at which four officers of U.S.S. *Wyoming* (which chanced to be moored in the next line) were present. There was a concert by the ship's company that evening, and after a delectable hour and a half of Anglo-Australian chaff and harmony had been brought to a close by the playing of "God Save the King" and the "Star Spangled Banner," the officers returned to the wardroom for a quiet hour with their pipes. The thing started, I believe, when somebody wound up the gramophone with a "Chu-Chin-Chow" record on it, and everybody joined in on the chorus. Then it transpired that the American guests showed unmistakable evidence of "team-work" in their harmony, and presently the others fell out and left the quartette singing alone. Two or three strange new "jazzy rags," which had not yet won their way to popular favour on this side of the Atlantic, gave way to "Mississippi" and "Tennessee" and the classic melody of "I've Been Working on the Railroad." Finishing up with a flourish in a snappily executed bit of "buck-and-wing-ing," the guests then insisted that they had occupied the centre of the stage long enough, and demanded that the next round of the show should be British.

The hosts, affirming that they could not think of producing an anti-climax by following on after so finished a musical performance as that just concluded, said they would nevertheless endeavour to provide their share of entertainment by playing a game of "chair polo." This spirited competition quickly resolved itself into a general rough-and-tumble, out of which the fatherly Major of Marines, who was the senior officer of the guests, only managed to keep one of the young American Lieutenants by reminding him that it was not becoming that an officer and gentleman should break furniture outside of his own ship.

When all the British officers had fought themselves into a state of collapse, a hulking young midshipman who was roosting precariously on two legs of the lounging chair under which the Commander was imprisoned, gave vent to his exultation by taking in a lungful of air and expending it in the blood-curdling Maori war-cry, which he had learned in his New Zealand home before he joined the Navy. That gave the visitors a chance to get in the running again, and, putting their heads close together and beating out the rhythm with their fists, they fairly started the rivets on the wardroom ceiling with the thunderous bark of the Navy yell. The Maori war-whoop was like the chirping of a cricket in comparison. Wide-eyed with wonder and admiration, the British officers relaxed the death grips in which they had been holding each other, and gathered near to see at close range how the big noise was made. The Gunnery Lieutenant slipped away for a moment, presently to reappear wearing his "ear-defenders." "Always use 'em when the big stuff is firing," he explained; "when do we start the next run?"

Nothing would do but that the officers of H.M.S. "——" should be taught the Yankee Navy yell. A class was formed then and there, and lessons were in full swing an hour later when the Officer of the Watch poked his head timidly inside the door to announce that the boat for the American officers had been standing-by for twenty minutes, but that he had been waiting for a pause in the singing to report it. He was a serious-looking little Sub, that Officer of the Watch, and I never could make quite sure whether he thought it was really singing (perhaps a new kind of Yankee ragtime) he was interrupting or not.

Ducking under hammocks in which restive would-be sleepers were stirring, we filed up the ladder and came out into the frosty air of the quarterdeck to speed the parting guests. Good-nights were spoken softly in deference to the Captain, whose sleeping cabin was just beneath our feet, and the four cloaked officers tip-toed gently down the gangway and aboard their waiting launch. Then the Commander passed a quietly spoken order down the line along the rail. "Ready now; altogether. One—two—three!"

With the sudden roar of a full gun salvo, the Navy yell boomed out on the still air and went rolling forth across the still waters to set strange echoes chattering in the distant hills. A sudden surge of quickly suppressed laughter floated back to us from the receding launch, but the visiting officers were on their good behaviour once they were "out in the open" again, and the challenge was not taken up.

The Commander was chuckling as he bade me good night in the half-darkness of the wardroom flat. "There can't have been such another yell as that heard by these quiet waters since they were first ploughed by the galleys of the old Norse Vikings," he said with a laugh. "I'd really like to know just how many of the fifty or sixty thousand men of the Grand Fleet awakened by it knew to what Navy that 'Nav-eee!' they heard referred to. Not that it makes much matter, though, now that we're all one."

II. WHAT THE BRITISH BLUEJACKET THINKS OF THE AMERICAN

The British naval officer, sapient of many ports and peoples, had a pretty clear idea that in the American Naval Officer he was going to find an ally who, in spite of a number of superficial differences from himself, would still be a deal easier to act in intimate co-operation with than any of those with whom he had been fighting up to the time of the entry of the United States into the war. With the British sailor it was different. Only a few of him had ever met any American bluejackets, and these meetings—for the most part confined to the bars and bunds of Shanghai, Hongkong, Singapore, and the other ports of the Far East—had not always been of a nature calculated to be promotive of international amity. The American Jackie was chiefly remembered by the British for the softness of a speech that belied the hardness of a fist, and an astonishing and unaccountable penchant for scattering Mexican dollars from rickshaws for coolies to scramble for.

It was a good deal as a brine-pickled old British man-o'-wars-man of many years' service said to me a few days ago. "We never had no chance to know the Yanks afore the present, sir. We was allus eyin' each other distrustful like when we was in the same ports, and we was never gettin' much closer than the length o' a bar apart. Result was that we only seed the few things in them that was diff'rent from what we was, and they likewise wi' us. And o' course we never spotted the things in which we was just alike. All that I rec'lect o' the Yanks we used to run into on the China Station was that they was dressed diff'rent from us, talked diff'rent, and even swore diff'rent. The way they cussed struck me most of all. It was so earnest like. That was the thing I remembered 'em best for—as the blokes wot cussed like they was sayin' their prayers."

And so it was that the British and American bluejackets remembered each other for their differences rather than for the traits they had in common. Naturally, the picture was a distorted one on both sides. But when, with the coming of the American ships to European waters, the first chance to get together and become really acquainted was offered, each soon began to see the other in the proper perspective, and from the very first they have become better and better friends with every day that went by.

A good many British sailors have told me during the last few months of the increasing ties of friendship and kinship that were knitting between them and the "Yanks," but perhaps some extracts from an article which has just appeared in the little monthly magazine published by the Lower Deck of one of the battleships of the Grand Fleet will give the best idea of the way things have gone in this respect. It was signed "Bluejacket," and I have learned that the writer is a Seaman Gunner who, like the great majority of his mates, never met any of his cousins from across the Atlantic until the American Battleship Squadron joined the Grand Fleet last winter.

"We had all heard a good deal of the Yankee Fleet," it begins, "and a few of us had seen Yankee ships before in our voyages abroad; but to the most of us their manners and customs were a sealed book; and so many curious glances were cast toward their battleships, after their arrival to take their place beside us, just to catch a glimpse of an American sailor. We all had our various ideas of what they were really like, and I am giving away no secret when I say that we did not expect them to come up to our standard, or to be very much our own kind. This was inevitable owing to the feeling fostered by some sections of the British press during the preceding years of the war in which America had been neutral. Consequently we were more than a little surprised on meeting them ashore for the first time to find them such very good fellows. Perhaps the thing that surprised us most about them was to find that there was less difference between the English that they talked than there was between that of the Cockney and the

Scotchman, or the Cornishman and the Yorkshireman, or the Welshman and the Lancashireman. That is to say, it was easier for the run of us to understand them than it was for us to understand each other. But the thing that we liked best about them was the quiet way they had of speaking. This, I must admit again, was also a great surprise to us, for the Yankee of our funny papers and music-halls was invariably very loud-mouthed and boastful. They had some rather fearful and wonderful slang, it is true, but the most of it was so expressive that we had not the least difficulty, first, in following it, and then beginning to adopt it for our own use. For instance, it was as easy to see that 'Some class, those shooting irons on the *Lizzie*,' referred to the 15-inch guns of the *Queen Elizabeth*, as it was to see that 'pretty nifty with his hot footing, hey bo?' referred to the way Charley Chaplin was kicking out with his feet in the movie (there, I have dropped into a 'Yankeeism' myself! Nothing could be more catching) at the Y.M.C.A. hut. We have probably been borrowing more of their language than they have of ours so far, for many of the Yankeeisms seem to go right to the spot so much better than ordinary English.

"Our first meetings on shore got on so well that we decided to get up some kind of a game with them. It was out of the question for us to try to play their baseball or football, just as it was for them to tackle our cricket. But we had heard that one of their ships had been having a try at our Association football, and on the strength of this we sent them a challenge for a game of 'Soccer.' The fact that they jumped at the chance to take us on at a game at which they had practically no experience at is the best evidence of the kind of sporting spirit we have found the Yanks showing about everything.

"When the time for the game came there is no denying that we began to get rather nervous; not because we were not sure we were going to give them a licking (for ours is the champion Soccer team of the Grand Fleet), but because we weren't quite sure what we were going up against. (There goes another Yankeeism, just because it puts the thing better than any words in our own language.) We had read of what a shambles the field at an American football game was, and of how the men fought in armour, like the knights of the crusades, and of how each team was attended by its own stretcher-bearers and casualty clearing station. Frankly, we were afraid that they might take the occasion to 'Yankefy' Soccer along these lines. As a precautionary measure, we made a point of getting shore leave for just as many men as possible, so as to be sure of being in sufficient force to back up our boys if it came to a fight for life. Indeed, we were much relieved to find on landing that the British bluejackets outnumbered the American by three to one, and that there were no evidences of hospital arrangements.

"Of course we beat them, for our team had years' experience of the game where theirs had days, but the game was keenly contested all the way, and the score of six to one in our favour was by no means as one-sided as we could have piled up against many of the British ships of the Grand Fleet. There was no sentiment about it, either. We licked them as bad as we could. Their training in the Yankee game had made them quick to master the main points of the British, and the result was that they had made a progress in the latter which must have been just about a record considering only one or two of them had ever seen Soccer before. We heard them cursing each other a bit now and then in an effort to stiffen up their defence, but so far as we were concerned they displayed nothing but the cleanest kind of sportsmanship. By their showing on this occasion we were prepared to hear, as we did shortly, that this same Yankee team had won games of Soccer from two or three of the British battleships and battle cruisers. Nothing but their greater interest in baseball, which they were able to take up in the spring, has prevented the Yanks from turning out a football team that would have been a real contender for the Grand Fleet championship, and even as it is they have given us an example of their adaptability, quick-wittedness, and sportsmanship that has won the admiration and respect of everybody.

"But it was not till the long days of summer came and shore leave was granted more liberally that we had a chance to really form friendships with our new allies. Perhaps it was baseball that helped us more than anything else in getting acquainted. The Commander-in-Chief having provided suitable grounds, a baseball league was formed of the teams of the several American battleships, and from the very start these games provided a very strong counter-attraction to our own football matches. There might be a half-dozen football games in progress, but the moment the wild yelling from down in front of the pavilion told that a baseball game was under weigh all the spectators melted away at once, and sometimes even the players themselves chucked their hands in and went over to see the antics of the Yanks. It was these antics—rooting, I think they call it, though I don't quite know why—that attracted us at first, but we were not long in finding out what they were driving at, and really following the progress of the game. Certainly none of us had ever seen the ball handled with such dexterity, both in the way it was caught and the way it was thrown, and the best cricket seemed dull and tame in comparison. We especially admired the quickness of the players on their feet, both in fielding and running round the bases. Few British bluejackets could show such speed, and we have decided the Yankees are faster because they are all shorter service men than we are, and so have had less time to get slow and beefy through ship life. We hope to make our beef and bulk tell against them in boxing and rowing. They tell us that it takes ten years to make a good baseball player, and we can well believe it. As none of us are yet ready to acknowledge the possibility of the war lasting that long, it is hardly likely that we shall try to turn out any teams with the idea of nosing the Yanks out of the baseball championship of the Grand Fleet, but all the same we are fully determined to tackle the game for the game's sake, and to play it among ourselves as we get a chance. The British matelot never did have the patience to play cricket, but baseball has so much that cricket lacks that it is by no means impossible that he may take to it in time, just as our Canadian cousins have. In the mean time our old song which goes 'We'll ramp and we'll roar like true British sailors' will have to be sung, 'We'll ramp and we'll roar like Yankee baseballers,' for there is no question that they can out-ramp and out-roar us with several cables'-lengths to spare.

"The baseball games have given us a welcome chance to show our friendship for the American bluejackets. It is the custom to provide each member of a British shore-leave party with tickets good for two pints of beer at the Recreation Club. The Yank ships, being teetotallers, did not do this, and so the poor chaps would have had to get on without any beer if we had not come to their rescue. Soon it became quite the regular thing for a British sailor to provide his Yankee chum with half his beer-tickets, and, as many of the days were sweltering hot, you may believe they were appreciated. As the present beer we get does not contain enough alcohol to intoxicate a fly, American mothers need have no fear that there is anything in this action calculated to lead their sailor boys astray.

"I need hardly say that the Yanks have reciprocated every time they had a chance. I was having tea at the Naval Club a few days, and, having neglected to bring any sugar ashore from the ship, I was about to do the best I could without it, when an American sailor reached over from the next table and handed me his ration, saying that he had come provided with an extra one for just that purpose. And it was fine white sugar, too. I have seen the same thing happen a number of times. The Yanks seem to be allowed an extra lot of sugar and sweets to make up for not having grog. They tell me that they don't miss the latter very badly, and I can't say that they seem any the worse for not having it. Perhaps that is the one thing that we have worried most about since the Yankees came—as to whether or not their example would cause the British ships to 'go dry' too. Who can say? Stranger things have happened, but the change will hardly come during the war anyhow.

"The few weeks' sport at this Base gave the men a chance to meet in such a way that they could form real friendships, and I know of a number of instances where British sailors have asked Yankees to visit them in their homes if ever there is a chance that the leaves work out favourable to that arrangement. We found that we had a great many things in common with them; so much so that, writing some weeks after these meetings, it seems awkward to speak of them as Yanks at all, they have become so much part and parcel of ourselves.

"I cannot close this without mentioning an amusing incident which occurred to a messmate of mine. This chap was told off for patrol duty at the railway station, and, as was usual, had a Yankee sailor as a partner, the latter being provided with a small truncheon, according to their custom. The British lad, who was a good deal of a youngster, got interested in the stick and asked many questions, to all of which the American replied with the greatest good humour. Among other things, he said that the truncheon was 'loaded,' and that it was used for quieting obstreperous sailors. After this my friend kept his distance, and on returning to his mess explained to an attentive crowd all the happenings of the afternoon, ending up by saying that he took no chances with that 'loaded gun' stick, as he was afraid it might go off by mistake. It appears that he actually thought that a 'loaded' stick meant one that 'went off' when a man was hit with it. You may be sure that we lost no time in passing the joke on to the Yanks, who appear to be enjoying it quite as much as we have. Indeed, perhaps the surest sign of the good solid base our friendship is built on is the fact that it has long ago reached the 'joking' stage—the one at which we both feel quite free to throw aside 'company manners' and 'rag' each other without fear of being misunderstood or hurting any one's feelings. And that, let me tell you, means that we've at last got out a sheet-anchor that ought to keep the barque of our common friendship head-to-wind through any storm that is ever likely to threaten to swamp it."

I do not think there is much that I need add to this naïve but comprehensive statement of the way in which the Yankee bluejacket has impressed his fellows of the British Navy. The life of the Grand Fleet is a strenuous one, and at times many weeks may go by in which there is no opportunity for the men to foregather ashore. How well these rare opportunities have been used by the British and American sailors to become acquainted is evidenced by the frequency with which the officers doing the ship's censoring come across letters from one to the other, and the cordiality of the feeling which is springing up may be judged by the fact that the commonest form of address is "Dear Chum." The friendships which are growing between the thousands of Americans and Britons who are holding the seas to-day will be of incalculable influence in strengthening the bonds of international amity between the two nations upon whom most of the responsibility will rest in determining the future of civilization.

III. What the American Bluejacket thinks of Britain and the British

The scroll of human experience has been unrolling at rather a dizzy rate for both the American soldier and sailor during the last year; but it has seemed to me to be the latter—probably because he has somewhat more time to "sit and think" than the former—that has gone the farthest in the orderly pigeon-holing of his impressions. All the spirit of the soldier's being has been concentrated on his preparation for "licking the Boche." In mind and body he is fitting himself for his grim task, and his outlook on life and things generally is not uncoloured by the red mist that is deepening before his eyes as the time of his big moment approaches. With the sailor it is different. Although, first and last, the part that he is playing and will play in winning through is every bit as important as that of the soldier, his hate of the Hun is rather more impersonal, and he is less inclined to have his moments of "seeing red" than is the Yankee soldier. It is this fact that has made the American sailor a rather more detached and unbiased observer of the things the war drama has unrolled before him than is the soldier.

"How do things look to you after a year of real war?" I asked a tall youth in blue jeans and a grey armless sweater whom I found tinkering with the sights of the forecastle gun of the destroyer in which I chanced to be out with for a few days at the time. The question was merely an ingratiating attempt to get acquainted on my part, and was ventured with no expectation of drawing a serious answer. I was not as familiar then as I have become since with the material they are making the young Yankee sailor of, however. He turned on me a keen eye, with wrinkles at the corners which I was quite right in surmising had come there through gazing at heat-waves dancing along broad horizons long before he had squinted down the sight of a naval gun. My diagnosis of "Texas cowboy" only missed the truth by the difference between that and an "Oklahoma oil driller, with a 'Varsity education and a ranch of his own."

He leaned back easily with an arm over the gun-breech (where a British bluejacket under similar circumstances would have stiffened at once to attention), and yet there was nothing familiar or disrespectful in his attitude. "It looks to me like two or three things," he said after a moment of wrinkling his tanned brow as he collected his thoughts. "It looks to me as though these waters hereabouts were not going to be exactly a happy hunting-ground for the U-boat now that we're beginning to savy the game good and proper. That's one thing. Another is, that it's beginning to look as if they're waking up to the fact in the States that to call a man 'politician' is one degree worse than to call him a ---- ———. It took them a year or two of war to learn that in England, and we didn't profit much by their example. Another thing—it looks like Americans—or at least those of us as have come across to this side—are going to have a fair chance to discover that the natives of these little islands are more or less the same kind of animals the Yanks are after all. We've never had that chance in the last hundred and forty years. Instead, we've been taught from our cradles to nurse a grudge that was really wiped out when we licked them—or such forces as they could send across then—and set up business on our own account in '76. And one more thing. It looks as if Americans were at last getting off their blinkers in the matter of the Irish; that they are beginning to understand that these—but, excuse me, sir" (he turned and started adjusting the sighting mechanism again), "I just saw the Captain come up on the bridge, and I don't like to swear too freely in his hearing. And a man can't talk about this end of Ireland—or leastways about the way it's acted in the war—without swearing."

These offhand observations come pretty near to epitomising the several salient ideas that have been crystallising in the mind of the American sailor in the course of his year or more of active service in the war. If he is in a destroyer or submarine operating against the U-boat he knows full well what has been done in turning the little neck of the Atlantic where he works into what may well be termed a "marine hell" for the pirates. If he is in one or the other of these branches of the service, too, the fact that he has based in a South of Ireland port has given him a liberal education in the affairs of that "disthreshful country" and stirred in him the deepest abomination of Sinn Fein, all it stands for, and all who stand for it. A growing impatience and distrust of all professional politicians is common to the officers and men of all the American ships on this side, and bodes as hopefully for the future as does a similar feeling that is becoming increasingly evident in both the British Army and Navy.

But most profound of all the emotions stirred in the breast of the American sailor by the war and the new knowledge the war has brought him is undoubtedly his awakening sympathy and admiration for the British and Great Britain. The picture the most of him brought over of the Briton was a sort of hazy composite built up of what his school histories told him about George the Third's soldiers, and of what he himself had seen of the Briton—as represented on the American stage and in the funny papers. If he was a man of two or three enlistments—and these, because of the great dilution of new men which has become imperative with the expansion of the Navy, are not encountered very often—the effect of the composite was heightened by a picture of the British bluejacket as the American had met him on the waterfront of this or that foreign port. It goes without saying that the incarnation of that kind of a composite didn't seem a very promising individual for the Yankee sailor to make friends with. This creature of fancy was a male, of course. What the female of the species was he had an even hazier idea, and that there was really nothing to speak of to differentiate her from the girl, sister, or mother he had left behind him he never dreamed. Considering that this is the way things looked to him at the outset—and the picture is not in the least exaggerated—one cannot but feel that the American sailor has made most gratifying progress in correcting his perspective in a comparatively limited time and with few opportunities.

The men of the American battleships of the Grand Fleet—always on guard at its isolated base, and able to grant scant and infrequent leave to any one serving in it—have had less chance to see the country and its people than have their mates of the destroyers and submarines, whose bases have been more convenient to England and with chances of leave turning up rather oftener. Their main, almost their only, point of contact, therefore, has been the British bluejacket. Everything considered, perhaps there could not have been a better one. No finer, and yet more fairly characteristic, cross-section of the British people could be revealed than that shown by the personnel of the Royal Navy, from stoker or seaman to Commander-in-Chief. There is no class by which the Briton himself should be prouder to be judged.

I have already written of the mixed feelings of curiosity and interest with which the British bluejackets awaited their first intimate meeting with the Yanks. It was no whit different on the part of the latter. With the Northern Base swept by its more or less unending succession of winter storms, there was not much chance for personal contact in the first few months after the Americans came over, and before better weather and lengthening spring days gave opportunity for inter-fleet visits and foregatherings ashore the men of both Navies had had a good many chances to see each other handling their ships. From that alone a deep mutual respect was born, and it was on that solid foundation that the present astonishingly friendly relations between the men of the two allied Navies is based. The British, with four years of war experience behind them, were doing things with their ships, quite in the ordinary course of the day's work, that the Americans had never reckoned on attempting save in emergency. The shooting and the general efficiency of the British ships under the arduous North Sea winter conditions deepened and broadened the respect and admiration of the Americans the more they saw of it, and the more they discovered the extent to which they would have to exert and outdo themselves to equal it. The feeling of the American bluejacket on this score was concisely but comprehensively expressed by an old Yankee man-of-war's-man—one of the few real veterans I have encountered on this side—with whom I had a yarn not long after the arrival of U.S.S. *New York*.

Coming in from a "big-gun-shoot," the American squadron had sighted a squadron of British battle cruisers carrying out a series of intricate manœuvres with destroyers at a speed which would have been reckoned as suicidal as late as a year or two ago, and which there is little doubt would not be attempted outside of the Grand Fleet even to-day. The sun-pickled phiz of the old sea-dog crinkled with a grin of sheer delight and wonder as the lean cruisers, each a mass of turrets, funnels, and tripod mast between tossing bow-wave and foaming wake, dashed in and out of the spreading smoke-screens with a unity of movement that might have been animated by the pull of a single string. Then, when to cap the climax the speeding warships opened up with their heavies and began to straddle a target that was teetering along on the edge of the skyline ten or twelve miles away, he gave his broad thigh a resounding slap and turned to me with:

"By cripes, things do move, believe me! I was on the *Oregon* when we chased old Cervera's ships up the Cuba coast in the Spanish war, and we were nigh to busting our boilers doing half the speed of them battle cruisers. And as for keeping station—it was just a case of devil take the hindmost. But these Johnnies here would go straight through a scrap just as they're playing that little game over there. By cracky, I takes off my hat to them. They're sure on the job, and you just bet that's good enough for us."

I think if I was asked to sum up very briefly just what the American bluejacket thinks of the ships of the Grand Fleet and the men who man them, I would simply quote those final words—"They're sure on the job, and you just bet that's good enough for us."

With this foundation of respect and admiration to stand on once established, there was little to worry about on the score of personal relations. Both of them were as bashful as children on the occasions of their first tentative inter-ship visits, but this quickly wore off when they found that they both spoke the same language, and it was not very far from that to the "pal-ling" stage. Then they began to box and play occasional games of "soccer" together, and, where either could not play the other's sport, to give attention to baseball or "rugger," as the case might be, with the idea of trying to find out for themselves what there really was in the other man's game. This is still going on, and British sailors with baseball bats and gloves, or Yankee tars with cricket bats and shin pads, are becoming commoner and commoner sights at the recreation grounds in the vicinity of the northern bases.

I have already told how the feeling of the British bluejacket for the Yankee "gob"—as the latter appears to like to be called—changed from one of aloof curiosity, through a mild sort of "liking," to active affection; and to describe how the Americans' feelings have run the same gamut would be merely to tell the story in reverse. But I cannot refrain from setting down the personal tribute of one "gob" in particular to British bluejackets in general, for, in its way, it is quite as typical as the words I have quoted respecting the old Yankee gunner's estimate of the Grand Fleet.

The "gob" in question had been born on or very near the Bowery, but seven years in the Navy had obliterated all traces but the accent. He was a stoker, and as the champion "light-heavy" of the American squadron was being put on in an occasional special bout in the course of the British squadron eliminations. In spite of the fact that the British box only three rounds, where the American Navy had been boxing six, and a number of other variations in rules, he had done extremely well, having lost but a single bout, and that by being slightly out-pointed. He was still nursing a black eye from this latter contest—in which his sportsmanlike conduct no less than his cleverness had won the admiration of every one present—when I asked him if he had been satisfied with the decision. "Poifickly," was the instant reply. "He had too much steam for me from the first gong; but I'll do better when I've woiked out a lil' longer to go the three 'stead o' the six round course. Wot do I tink o' the British as sports? Say, they's the best ever. They's more than just gent'men. They's reg'lar fellers, take it from me, and wot more can you ask than that?"

If the Yankee sailor has any superlative beyond "regular feller" to apply to a mate who has met with his approval, I have yet to learn what it is.

The men of the American destroyers and submarines, working more by themselves than the battleships with the Grand Fleet, have seen rather less of the British bluejacket, and—with better opportunities for London leave—more of the British civilians than their mates in the latter units. They have all found much to entertain and interest them in Liverpool, London, Glasgow and the other large cities they have visited. They have enjoyed the theatres and art galleries, and are very appreciative of the various canteens that have been provided for their comfort. But it has been none of these that has made the greatest appeal to them, but rather those at first rare but now increasingly frequent visits to an English or a Scottish home. I don't mean the boat-on-the-river-with-band and the tea-party-on-the-lawn-of-some-ancestral-castle kind of thing, which are all very well as far as they go; but rather the quiet, unostentatious hospitality of a British home of somewhere near the same class as the visitor comes from in the States. This kind of kindness has gone straight to the heart. The Yankee sailor lad is a good deal more of a "mother's boy" than he will ever admit to any one save possibly some other boy's mother, and I have heard two or three pretty swaggery young "gobs" speak with rather more than a suggestion of a catch in their voices of the kindness that has been shown them—of the things they have seen and heard and learned—in one of these visits to a British home.

One day a quartermaster—his folding bed was triced up next to mine in the forward torpedo-flat, and we had fallen into the habit of exchanging confidences in the long quiet hours of submergence—of the American submarine in which I was recently out on its regular North Atlantic patrol told me how much the visit he had been privileged to make to a little English home in Liverpool had meant to him. And presently, after a pause, as though the thought of one had awakened the thought of the other in his mind, he told me of something else he had seen on one of his leave trips.

"I happened to be in Cork for a few hours on my way through," he said. "We are not allowed to visit there, you know, for fear that we may be tempted to beat up a few Sinn Feiners; but if we are marooned there waiting for a connexion there is nothing against our strolling about the town. Well, just at one end of the main bridge across the River Lee, they have the Stars and Stripes and the Union Jack floating side by side from the top of one of the iron poles of the electric car line. I don't know whose idea it was, except that the Sinn Feiners had nothing to do with it. Now the ordinary way to have handled them would have been to bend each flag to separate halyards, and to hoist and lower independently. But some man with a head on his shoulders (possibly he had been a sailor) evidently had the run of the show, and what had been done was this: Taking two crosspieces, he had bent the flags to the two lines joining their ends. Then a single halyard, rigged to run over a block to the upper crosspiece, hoisted and lowered the two flags, always side by side, at one operation. Well, now, looking at that, it chanced that I seemed to see something more than a very neat little contrivance for saving time in handling a couple of squares of coloured bunting. It seemed to me that it stood for a sort of symbol of the fact that the Stars and Stripes and the Union Jack are being rigged to fly together for a good many years; and that they aren't going to be able to lower one without bringing down the other."

I do not know how many of the men of the American ships at the Irish bases have seen that particular little "bunting hoist," but I do know that the sentiment my young submarine friend read into it finds an echo in the breast of practically every one of them.

Milton Keynes UK
Ingram Content Group UK Ltd.
UKHW040839141024
449705UK00006B/369